S0-BHV-489

Global E-Commerce Strategies for Small Businesses

Global E-Commerce Strategies for Small Businesses

Eduardo da Costa

LIBRARY
FRANKLIN PIERCE COLLEGE
RINDGE, NH 03461

The MIT Press
Cambridge, Massachusetts
London, England

©2001 Massachusetts Institute of Technology

All rights reserved. No part of this book may be reproduced in any form by any electronic or mechanical means (including photocopying, recording, or information storage and retrieval) without permission in writing from the publisher.

This book was set in Sabon by Best-set Typesetter Ltd., Hong Kong.

Printed and bound in the United States of America.

Library of Congress Cataloging-in-Publication Data

Costa, Eduardo da.
  Global e-commerce strategies for small businesses / Eduardo da Costa.
    p. cm.
  Includes bibliographical references and index.
  ISBN 0-262-04190-1 (hc.: alk. paper)
  1. Electronic commerce. 2. Small business. I. Title.
  HF5548.32 .C677   2001
  658.8′4—dc21

00-048965

To Nando, *amigão*, and Ticha, lifelong companion, my sources of inspiration and well being.

Contents

Preface

The Internet and its users today is comparable to sex and adolescents: everyone talks about it, but few have fully experienced it. Many people have used e-mail, the exchange of electronic mail (a very modest capability). But the Net's most significant applications are emerging slowly. Electronic commerce (e-commerce) is one of them. Goods and services will increasingly be traded online. Many consumers "window shop" on the Net and then buy goods at a retail store. But many others buy on the Internet and pay for the goods online. In fact, some goods can actually be delivered online. What kinds of products will be affected by e-commerce? More to the point, which products and services will not be affected? The unavoidable truth is that a new information society is dawning and every business must be prepared for it.

Why should small companies that are doing well in their local markets bother with exports at all? Because success in today's marketplace can be misleading. If the owners of small companies do not think globally, they may not be prepared when one of their local or international competitors begins to encroach on their local markets. Consumers already are buying services—from theater tickets to travel packages—directly on the Net. How does this change affect anyone's market?

Global E-Commerce Strategies for Small Businesses explains these rapidly changing times, signs of which are evident everywhere. Shares of Internet-related companies, even after some market correction, are being offered and traded on Wall Street at prices that are justifiable only if spectacular growth is anticipated. New forms of electronic commerce are being invented that will allow for small-change transactions ("a picture for a dime") that were simply nonexistent before. Teachers are surprised to learn details about their own subject from their pupils (who got them from the Net). And all these changes are happening very fast.

In this evolving scenario, what is the role of small companies? What opportunities are opening up for them in the global market? Are young entrepreneurs and small-company owners aware of the growing importance of their businesses for their local communities, their countries, and the world?

Global E-Commerce Strategies for Small Businesses examines opportunities in the global market for startup, small, and medium-size companies within the information industry or in any business sector. By recognizing opportunities and effectively using services provided by the information industry, owners and managers of small and medium-size companies, entrepreneurs in the making, teachers and students of the Internet, and professionals and other individuals who are considering starting a new company can reach the global market and thrive there.

The book describes seven successful small companies from six different countries in seven different kinds of businesses. Their most striking common characteristic is that the Internet and other information technologies were the very reason for their growth. The businesses range from an orchid producer and exporter in Singapore to a small eyeglasses shop in Italy to an electronic trading company in the United States. From their experiences you can learn what it takes to go global, but more important, you will realize that *it is now possible* for you too to trade internationally.

The export business may not be for everyone. A small bakery nestled in a quiet residential area anywhere in the world is not a likely exporter. But even a small shop of this kind can benefit from the information provided here. Think, for instance, about the items that a bakery buys: Are they available online? Can they be bought directly? Could several bakeries build an alliance to get a bulk discount when importing basic supplies? And once the bakers become familiar with the new medium, could they sell their packaged cookies abroad?

Although *Global E-Commerce Strategies for Small Businesses* is not intended as a how-to book about going online, it describes in detail all the steps necessary to start an international business. Once readers understand the procedure and the challenges involved, they will be in a better position to assess the status of their business as a potential global company.

The book is organized in two blocks. The first (chapters 1 through 4) provides a context for decision making with background information on small companies, on the information industry and the evolution of electronic commerce, and on the challenges of going international. The second (chapters 5 through 8) describes examples of successful small companies worldwide and the lessons learned from their experience, gives an overview of the steps necessary for setting up a global business, and concludes with an optimistic view of things to come.

This conclusion goes beyond the business world to examine how information technologies will affect our social lives and our families. It describes my particular vision of the future—a time when small companies will have a much larger share of economic activity worldwide, when businesses and consumers will organize themselves into virtual communities, and when the world will be, quite simply, better.

Cambridge, Massachusetts

Acknowledgments

This book would not have been possible without contributions and support from many people and institutions. I thank them all from my heart. In particular, I would like to make the following acknowledgments:

To the Program on Information Resources Policy (PIRP) at Harvard University, my host for the duration of the work. The expert advice and encouragement from Prof. Tony Oettinger and John LeGates since the first drafts have been invaluable. Mary Walsh, Maria White, Claire Merola, and Ellin Sarot provided the necessary support and made day-to-day life much more pleasant. Ben Compaine provided me with most of the ideas and concepts in chapter 2, and I am especially grateful to him for his contribution.

To my companies NEST-Boston and i-cubo and all of their employees, especially Sergio Andrade, who conducted the research for the three case studies in Europe; Fernando Guimarães, who wrote earlier pieces for inclusion in chapter 4; and Clarice Wolowski, who contributed on earlier pieces for chapter 4 and researched figures, illustrations, and tables for inclusion in the book. Clarice also prepared the manuscript for printing.

To several people in different countries who helped in the research for the international case studies: old friends Monica and Roberto Pinheiro in Singapore; Sylvie Feindt of the KITE project in Europe; Frank Roche and Noelie Hanan in Ireland; Giusepe and Simone Monforte of the Export Consortia in Italy; Thomas Hopcroft, president of the Mass Ecomm Association in Boston; and Kival Weber, president of the SOFTEX Society in Brazil.

Thanks also to old friend Fernando Dolabela for his contributions to chapter 6. To Josephine Roccuzzo for the early editing of some of the chapters. To Susan Witt and Heather Davidson of the Schumacher Society in Great Barrington, who were so kind in helping me with research in the Schumacher Society library and in setting the perfect environment in which to write the book's last chapter.

To the MIT Press, which had the wisdom to identify the importance of the book's theme and the agility to turn the manuscript into print in a short time, a necessary condition to bringing such a timely subject to market. Special thanks to Elizabeth Murry, Deborah Cantor-Adams, and Vicki Jennings, who guided me through the publishing process.

Last, but in a very special place, to my family, Patricia and Nando, who are and have been great in coping with the stresses associated with the production of a book. I cannot thank them enough for what they both represent in my life. Nicky and Rodolfo, our two dogs, have also kept me company in some of the long nights at home.

My apologies to people I might have missed in this long list of contributors; my thanks go out to them too.

Global E-Commerce Strategies for Small Businesses

1

The Growing Worldwide Importance of Small Companies

A worm can roll a stone
A bee can sting a bear
A fly can fly around Versailles
'Cos flies don't care!
A sparrow in a hat
Can make a happy home
A flea can bite the bottom
Of the Pope in Rome!
—*Les Misérables*

A Common Misconception (or Size Isn't Everything)

Owners of small businesses the world over have traditionally labored independently—often in relative obscurity and on shoestring budgets—and their role in industry and society has largely been viewed as marginal. The social and economic contributions of small businesses have been overshadowed by the industry presence and financial muscle of large corporations. One of today's most common misconceptions is that large corporations are more important players—in both the business world and the community at large—than small businesses.

Imagine a cocktail party where three people meet for the first time. Typically, one of the first topics of their conversation is work:

"What do you do?"
"I'm a financial analyst for Citibank. And you?"
"I'm a marketer for Microsoft. What about you, Joe?"
"Well, I just have a small business here in town, you know."

Such self-effacement is common among small-company owners. Most of them are not aware that small companies are generating the majority of new jobs, innovative ideas, and economic development in the world today, as will be discussed here. Rather than feeling apologetic, Joe should realize that his social role is in a way even more important than that of either of his new acquaintances, the corporate climbers.

The misperception is magnified by the merger mania of the past few years. News of the latest megamerger hits the headlines almost every day: Citibank joins forces with Travelers Group, Mercedes with Chrysler. America Online (AOL) buys Time Warner (is it not the other way round?).[1] With the growing number of mergers between big companies, many business owners feel that small companies are becoming even less significant. After all, "If Digital had to join with Compaq to compete in the global market, who am I to even think of trying?"

The truth behind these megamergers, however, is that big companies are becoming bigger but also fewer, whereas small companies are growing in number and importance every day. Large firms are important players and are responsible in many cases for the very existence of small firms, since they require and help to establish a network of vendors and suppliers. But while large companies are generating output, small companies are creating jobs. For many countries and regions of the world, adequate employment is a critical need, and establishing an environment that nurtures the development of small companies has become a top priority.

The role played by small companies in the international market is another area of misconception. There is a general belief that the international market is the realm of large corporations. Owners of small companies that define the limits of their territory by town or state boundaries may have difficulty envisioning how they could enter other states' (or other countries') markets. For many other small companies, though, the data show a different picture. According to the U.S. Department of Commerce, U.S. exports grew at three times the rate of any other economic activity in the country, and half of the growth was attributable to small and medium-size enterprises (SMEs). Small companies have traditionally tended to focus on one product or service for the local market, but now many small companies are increasingly targeting the global market for that same market segment. John Naisbitt calls this trend "the global paradox" in his best-selling book by the same name.[2]

Information technology (IT) plays a large role in the global expansion of small businesses, but it is not the only factor. The trend toward globalization of the economy has been with us for several decades, since well before the Internet phenomenon, and has affected SMEs as well. But because of the Internet and e-commerce, small companies are an increasingly powerful driving force in the emerging global marketplace, creating new jobs and spurring innovation and economic development all over the world.

What Is a "Small Company"?

The definition of *small company* varies from country to country. In the United States, small companies are defined as having fewer than 100 employees; by that definition there are 25 million small U.S. companies. But because most of these small companies are the various business entities of a single owner, the number of small companies with at least one employee (other than the owner) is only between 5 and 6 million.

Americans define SMEs (including medium-size companies) as firms having fewer than 500 employees, but this definition is not useful statistically in Europe, since 99.9 percent of all European businesses fit that definition.[3] In fact, the snapshot of company size in Europe in 1992 shown in table 1.1 illustrates that the vast majority of the companies are run by the owner either alone or with up to nine employees.

Table 1.1
Number of Companies in Europe by Size, 1992

	Size of Company (number of employees)	Number of Companies (thousands)
One-person businesses	—	7,846
Microenterprises	1–9	6,783
Small enterprises	10–49	971
Medium-size enterprises	50–249	146
Large enterprises	More than 250	31

Source: European Parliament (1997).[3]

Table 1.2
Classification of Business Size in the three Major Economic Region

Employees	United States	Europe	Japan[a]
0–9	Micro	Micro	Micro
10–19	Micro	Small	Micro
20–49	Micro	Small	SME
50–99	Small	Medium	SME
100–249	Medium	Medium	Large
250–499	Medium	Large	Large
500 and up	Large	Large	Large

Sources: U.S. Small Business Administration (1999), European Parliament (1997), National Federation of Small Business Associations (1998).[5]
a. In Japan, commerce and service industries are micro if they have no more than five employees; retail industries are SMEs if they have no more than 50 employees; manufacturing and mining industries are SMEs if they have no more than 300 employees.

Small companies in developing countries are even more difficult to characterize, since less information is available and circumstances are more varied. In Korea, for instance, more than 2 million SMEs (companies having fewer than 300 employees) account for 50 percent of the total value added of the economy, 69 percent of the total workforce, and (most surprisingly) 43 percent of the annual exports.[4] In Indonesia, SMEs (companies making less than $5 million in income) employ 88 percent of the workforce and produce 39 percent of the country's output (although only 14 percent of the exports). Similarly, in Mexico, SMEs (companies having fewer than 300 employees) employ 78 percent of the workforce and produce 43 percent of the country's output but less than 20 percent of the exports.

Comparison of these numbers on an international level is difficult. Table 1.2 summarizes the definitions of business size in the three largest economic regions in the world.[5]

Definitions vary, but for the purposes of this discussion, microenterprises are companies with one to nine employees, and SMEs in general (including the microenterprises) are companies with fewer than 100 employees, unless otherwise stated.

Genesis of the Small Company

We are living in a time of rapid change. This thought was probably expressed frequently during both the nineteenth and twentieth centuries and perhaps before. Are things really that different now? Perhaps the most obvious difference is that the rate of change is increasing. We are being bombarded with new technologies and products that affect our daily lives. But because people tend to adapt to new technologies fairly quickly, we soon behave as though they have been around forever. Think of photocopiers, initially launched by Xerox. How did we get along without them? Many of us are old enough to have used mimeograph machines and carbon paper, but we tend to forget about such obsolete items. Even the ubiquitous PC that we now take for granted was launched in 1981, only two decades ago.

The Internet, one of the major driving forces in the market today, has been in widespread use for only a few years and commercially only since 1994. An important study about small companies, published by the White House in 1995, states that "the next decade will see an increase in the connectivity between and among organizations and markets" but does not even mention the word *Internet*.[6] So the commercial Internet, which will foster the international growth of small companies, is only in its toddler stage today. As it matures and realizes its full potential, the Internet is capable of generating excitement and attracting a lot of attention. The climate of change at this particular point in time is particularly conducive to the birth of new companies—especially small ones. Massive restructuring occurred in large organizations in the 1980s, followed by sometime dramatic downsizing in the 1990s. The American giant General Electric, for instance, quadrupled its output from $20 billion to $80 billion in the past twenty years—and *reduced* its workforce by 40 percent at the same time. Traditionally, employees of large corporations—big household names like AT&T, NTT, Philips, or IBM, as well as the large banks and public utilities—thought that the implied social contract of previous decades still was in force. The assumption was that hard work, commitment, and loyalty from the worker would be rewarded by the company with lifelong employment and generous fringe benefits, including a good pension plan. A two-decade awakening to the realities of modern corporate life has caused many bitter and disillu-sioned workers to weigh the advantages of working for large corpora-tions, working for small companies, and even being self-employed. This change in the corporate climate and the response of the workforce have increased the number of small companies today.

Startups are enormously varied and can have country-specific and even generation-specific characteristics. Here are a few examples.

The Entrepreneur with a New Idea

Entrepreneurs with new ideas are one of the main sources of new development. People often start companies after having an idea for a product they need and cannot find. Then an individual or a group devises a new product, a new service, or a new application for an exist-ing product or service. Ideas don't have to be revolutionary, as long as no one has thought of them before (or patented them yet). Many tele-phone companies were trying to develop electronic speech-recognition systems in the 1970s to implement a collect-call system with no live operators. The machine would have to understand the words *yes* and *no* from the called party in a collect call and either complete or cancel the call. An engineer in a small town in Brazil came up with the idea of the machine playing a recorded message saying, "This is a collect call from a person who will identify himself after this message. If you do not want to pay for the call, please hang up." This system is being used by several telephone companies today and generates billions of dollars in revenues. It involves no expensive machinery and is very simple. Examples like this usually make entrepreneurs ask, "Why didn't I think of this and patent it?"

The Investor Who Sees a Market Opportunity

Some people are looking for promising small businesses as investment opportunities. Market opportunities are everywhere. There's an old story about two shoe salesmen, an optimist and a pessimist, who were sent to a remote region only to find that the local population does not wear shoes. The pessimist reports back, "No business here. No one wears shoes." The optimist, on the other hand, reports back, "Huge market. Totally unexplored so far."

An important source of new companies is individuals or groups that can spot a market opportunity and invest money to take advantage of it. A packaged version of the search for market opportunities can be found in the franchise scheme. The fast-food chains, for instance, have devised models that help franchisees identify the right spot for a new facility—number of passing cars, average income in the region, availability of other fast-food stores in the area, and so on. With these numbers in hand, someone with money available for investment and an interest in opening a business can write a business plan and decide whether to proceed with the new enterprise.

The Small Services Provider

Many people start by working alone and offering their services individually and then, as their clientele and the business grow, add a staff to organize the scheduling of services, the purchase of materials, and other aspects of their expanding business. This scenario is typical for household and office service providers such as plumbers, electricians, gardeners, and maintenance providers. In some countries, medium to large companies prefer to contract out all of these ancillary services to avoid contract disputes with trade unions and other forms of organized labor. Personal health-care services constitute another sector that will experience a boom in the coming years as the population ages.

The Jobless Person Who Sees No Alternative

Although this group is the least likely to succeed in the market, many people start their own companies as an employment alternative after not succeeding in a series of attempts to find or hold a job in a company. After running their own business for a time, many return eventually to a paid position under an employer. But many discover a new interest and go forward with the new company. In fact, the number of years that a typical worker spends in the same job tends to diminish over time. Not only does the number of different jobs in a worker's lifetime tend to increase, but the sequential combination of paid jobs, entrepreneurship, partnerships with other small companies, and other business options also tends to increase.

The Middle-Aged "Downsized" Manager

Large corporations have gone through a reengineering process over the last few decades that often drastically restructured their businesses and generally cut their workforce, sometimes by a large percentage. The process of downsizing usually starts when employees are offered some type of "voluntary" leave, and straight dismissals follow. During the voluntary-leave phase, some seasoned managers view the opportunity as the extra push they needed to start their own companies. Those who take this initiative are the most likely to succeed in their new ventures. Those who are involuntarily dismissed may also try something new but are likely to opt for the more traditional approaches, such as opening a new shop of a well-known franchise such as Benetton or Burger King.

The Retired Couple Finding a New Interest

Life expectancy is increasing in many parts of the world, and many people desire an active work life after retirement. Some of them may open small shops or run small businesses from home, using the new telecommunications technologies. They may do it for fun or to supplement retirement incomes. As the older population becomes better acquainted with computers, their opportunities to run small businesses will become even greater. There is already evidence of business ventures—traditional businesses or Internet businesses[7]—that cater to the needs of this specific age cohort.

Life Cycle

There are several classical descriptions of the evolution of a small company.[8] But the sheer number and variety of companies, patterns of growth, business options, and cultures around the world make it nearly impossible to anticipate the development of small businesses in general. This book focuses on small-company owners who want to use the Internet to reach the international market. The life cycle presented here matches the evolution of Internet-oriented small companies but may be useful as an approximation for those in our target audience.

Table 1.3
The Growth of a Start-Up Company

Milestones	Idea	Launch	Angel	Structure	IPO
Stages	Development	Organization	Growth	Consolidation	
People	1–2	2–6	4–10	8–20	
Period (months)	2–6	4–6	6–12	6–24	
Total cost (in $1,000s)	20–40	200–300	500–1,000	800–2,000	
Revenues (in $1,000s)	0	40–100	200–500	500–2,000	

The five milestones—and four stages between them—in the initial phase of a startup company are shown in table 1.3. The milestones include the following:

Idea   An individual or a small group has an idea about how to make money with a new business or with an adaptation of an existing business.

Launch   The business starts to operate in the market (opens its doors, launches a Web site, or starts calling on potential customers, for example).

Angel   The now established business has a few clients and small revenues and manages to attract the first round of capital, usually from an "angel investor."[9]

Structure   The company's structure has to be changed now. Someone is taking care of finance and administration, a proper office is set up, and roles are better defined.

IPO   A real company is now in the market. Growth is slower and depends much more on heavy capital investment. It is now time for the second round of financing, sometimes through an initial public offering (IPO).

The four stages (see table 1.3) include development, organization, growth, and consolidation. Development occurs between the idea and launch milestones: it is the stage when the product or service is improved so that it can be launched in the market. This stage can take a couple of people between two to six months and costs mostly the salaries of the developers. No revenues are earned. Growth occurs when developers use the money received in the first round of financing to hire people and revenues start to flow. During the organization stage, costs start to be matched by revenues. And in the fourth stage, consolidation occurs as the new company becomes a real company with an organization, some structure, and maybe some profits. Market share becomes a worry, and marketing efforts tend to be costly. This stage continues until the second round of financing, which can come in different forms. One of them is the IPO, as explained above.

On the road from idea to IPO many businesses disappear. The infant mortality of new businesses is high. In the developed world, the proportion of survivors after four years on average is around half, ranging from 36 percent in the United Kingdom to nearly 70 percent in Germany or Denmark.[10] But these numbers do not necessarily reflect the failure of those businesses that do not survive. Some companies are successfully sold, and some owners switch from one kind of business to another or from one kind of organization to another.

Entrepreneurship

The study of entrepreneurship is not new. A book called *Self-Help* by Samuel Smile, published in Britain in 1859, described the positive traits of self-made men such as James Watt (inventor of the steam engine), Richard Arkwright (cotton mills), and Josiah Wedgewood (potteries). The book sold 250,000 copies, an amazing best seller for that time. Recently, a British think-tank group produced a study that showed that economic development followed every period of rapid proliferation of new companies.[11] Other countries have also noticed this fact and are trying to foster entrepreneurship, with an eye toward supporting the development of new companies. But who is an entrepreneur, and what is an entrepreneurial venture?

Peter Drucker, in his best-selling book *Innovation and Entrepreneurship*,[12] made the distinction between a new standard small business and the new entrepreneurial company. If you decide to open a new bakery in your neighborhood, you are surely taking risks—perhaps less so if you follow the instructions of a good franchise chain. But are you an entrepreneur? Not by Drucker's definition. Drucker defines *entrepreneur* as one who "shifts resources from areas of low productivity and yields to areas of higher productivity and yield." This capability is not a personality trait. Perhaps the essential entrepreneurial qualities are the ability to live with uncertainty and the ability to make decisions. In fact, according to Drucker, people who do not have these characteristics will not do well as entrepreneurs—but they will also probably not do well in other activities, such as politics or aircraft command.

The conditions necessary to start a new business that is truly entrepreneurial vary, of course, but Joshua Hyatt[13] proposes this checklist:

New idea	Is your idea good enough? Will consumers really want what you're offering? Are investors likely to invest in it?
Value of money	How important to you is the potential financial reward from the company's success?
Risk taking	Are you willing to take some risks? Are you prepared perhaps to lose some of your money at the beginning?
Family backing	Are you aware of the commitment of time and energy that the new venture will demand of you? Have you thought about its effect on your personal life and family duties? Does your family support you in this endeavor?

Governments in many regions of the world have recognized the importance of fostering the entrepreneurial skills of students at different levels of the learning ladder, not only in universities but also before and after that time. In England, the British prime minister is lending his official support to a proposal to teach entrepreneurship at high schools for students ages thirteen to seventeen. These experiences are crucial to students who might otherwise assume that their only employment option is to work for someone else's company throughout their professional careers.

I once conducted a survey among my computer science students in Brazil and asked two questions: In what type of environment would you like to conduct your professional life? Where do you think you will actually work? Their answers varied, but the results were surprising. Overall what they wanted most was to work in their own company, but overwhelmingly they thought that instead they would end up working for a large local or multinational corporation. This survey was taken a few years ago, but large companies were already restructuring and downsizing. The only explanation I could fathom is that university lecturers probably had the idea that they were preparing their students to be good employees and didn't even consider that their students would rather run their own companies.

Innovation

Innovation is surprisingly difficult to define. It is related to novelty, ideas, invention, and change. But beyond that, it must have value to someone.

Most inventions do not lead to innovative products or services. But innovations can be related to processes, not only to tangible objects. So an innovation could be a new product, a new service, or a new way of doing something that is perceived by the user as inventive and valuable. It can be very complex or extremely simple. A good example is the launching of the automated collect call in Brazil in the 1970s described earlier in this chapter.

Companies of any size can produce innovations, but smaller companies tend to produce more of them. This is because in large corporations innovations encounter the following obstacles:

• Innovations may compete with existing products. Competition affects the power structure within a corporation and may be preemptively aborted by the affected party.

• Innovations may have only a small window of opportunity. By the time every managerial level in a corporation has had the time to analyze a new product or process, the opportunity may have passed.

• Innovations need time for development. In a corporation, development time competes with assigned tasks, and approval to do something unplanned and unfamiliar has to go through management channels, so innovative ideas often languish and die.

In the United States, according to the U.S. Small Business Administration (SBA),[14] 55 percent of all innovation is attributable to small companies. This doesn't mean that innovation doesn't occur in large corporations. They have tried to tackle the problem in several different ways with varying degrees of success. Digital Equipment Corporation (DEC), for instance, was an innovator when it pioneered the minicomputer revolution (a computer in each department) but then missed both the microcomputer revolution (a computer on every desk) and the server revolution and ended up being swallowed by a successful younger company (Compaq). IBM, on the other hand, missed the minicomputer revolution but launched the personal computer (PC) revolution in 1981 and is the first large company to highlight the importance of e-commerce in shaping the future of the computer industry.

Because of their size, density, and hierarchical structure, large corporations may need to devise methods to tackle the obstacles to innovation. Innovative ideas may be hidden somewhere deep in the organization and never see the light of day. In small companies, however, innovation can happen more spontaneously. The structure is more transparent, workers share ideas more freely, and the innovator may be able to talk directly with the person in charge of research and development.

Job Creation and Economic Development

Many people believe that worthwhile jobs exist only in large corporations "because salaries are higher," which tends to be true, and "because the jobs are secure," which is a myth. Large companies have been reducing their numbers of employees for several reasons:

- To reduce costs and become more competitive,
- To follow the latest management trend (for example, reengineering),
- To shake up the company (as, for instance, new CEOs often do),
- To improve the relation between revenues and the number of employees by subcontracting some of the work (which doesn't change the numbers much), and
- To get rid of old managers and staff.

The recent merger mania among large companies has exacerbated this trend. The initial statement by each CEO in any merger between two companies often is, "We are not planning any job cuts at this stage," followed within the next two years by severe job cuts, which were certainly a part of the merger plan from the beginning.

So large companies generally are not generating new jobs; small companies—and in particular, new small companies—are. In Europe, for example, there are 18 million SMEs, and they employ 66 percent of the workforce.[15] Additionally, 2 million small companies start up every year, and they are a major force in job creation.[16] The mortality rate of very young SMEs is high, but even though between 9 and 10 percent of these companies disappear every year, the net increase of around 300,000 new companies in Europe per year is still impressive.

Small businesses are especially concentrated in services and technology—the fastest-growing business sectors in the global economy—and therefore the areas that tend to achieve higher growth rates and economic development in general. In the United States, small businesses account for approximately 50 percent of the country's gross domestic product (GDP). Most strikingly, small businesses have provided virtually all of the nearly 20 million net new jobs added to the economy since 1992.[17]

The 24 million small businesses in the United States employ 53 percent of the private workforce. The businesses involved with the international market generate even more jobs per revenues: it is estimated that for every $1 billion in exports, 20,000 new jobs are created.

In developing countries, the need for support in fostering small companies is particularly pressing. In many parts of the world, the best jobs (at least as perceived by the majority of the population) are in the government and are not entrepreneurial. According to a World Bank report published in 1997, the big five developing countries (Brazil, China, India, Indonesia, and Russia), which accounted in 1997 for 8 to 10 percent of the world's output and trade, would double that figure by 2020.[18] Although large corporations and state-related enterprises will spur some of this development, most of it will come from small companies, and those businesses will be generating desperately needed new job opportunities. Technology will help. According to J. A. Kargbo, "There is no overstating that there is vast potential for businesses in developing countries on the Internet."[19]

Lack of Technology and Other Problems in Small Companies

Slow Penetration of Technology

The degree of penetration of modern information technologies in small companies is not very great worldwide. Microcomputers are widespread, but they are used mostly for routine tasks such as editing, formatting, and creating spreadsheets. In Europe in 1997, for instance, 98 percent of large corporations had access to the Internet, but only 4 percent of the SMEs did.[20] In the United States, the growth has been dramatic. The Yankee Group found that in 1998 only 28 percent of companies with fewer than twenty employees maintained a Web presence. By the end of the 1990s, though, among 7.4 million active U.S. small businesses 4.2 million had access to the Net, representing a penetration of 57 percent. Almost 17 million of 68 million small-business employees used the Internet, and spending on online transactions and purchases grew more than 1,000 percent, rising from $2 billion in 1998 to $25 billion in 1999.[21]

The situation is changing rapidly in the developed world, but the huge potential that the new technologies represent is still largely untapped by small companies in the rest of the world. There are several reasons for this slow penetration. One is a lack of awareness of (or a reluctance to accept) technological changes. The rate of acceptance of new technologies may vary from country to country, even in the developed world. Americans are more likely to take risks and try new technologies than Europeans are. Among Europeans, the Scandinavians are much more willing to adopt telecommunications novelties, and as a result there is a higher percentage of wireless phone and Internet users in these countries than anywhere else in the world.

Another reason for the slow penetration of technology is the relatively high cost of up-front investment and telecommunications technology. In the United States, local phone calls are not charged by time usage, and hours of Internet use cost the same as a local call—a maximum 35 cents per call. But in European countries, India, and Brazil, for example, the cost of connection time alone can be prohibitive for a small company. With the increase in competition for local phone services in some countries, however, these prices tend to drop. For some countries, overcoming these difficulties is seen as crucial: the United Kingdom has created a cabinet post for an e-minister who is charged with finding solutions to these types of problems and with educating small company owners about the importance of the technological revolution:[22] "As SMEs are so pivotal to the U.K. economy, it may be that the route to achieving the Information Society will be through winning the hearts and minds of SME management."[23]

Venture Capital

Many people believe that the venture-capital (VC) industry[24] is widespread throughout the developed world, but this is not true. Although there has been some VC activity in Europe in the past few years,[25] it is mostly an American phenomenon—at least for VC companies that are willing to invest in startups with high risk. The Mecca of the VC industry is really Sand Hill Road in Palo Alto, California, and not the large financial centers in London, Tokyo, or even New York. Business failure is socially regarded differently in different countries. According to *The Economist*: "If you start up a company in London or in Paris and go bust, you have just ruined your future. Do it in Silicon Valley, and you have just completed your entrepreneurial training."[26]

Management

SMEs are notorious for having managerial problems—primarily because most owners are not managers by training or vocation. Successful entrepreneurs have many relevant skills, but few are proficient in all the necessary business functions. Empirical estimates reported by M. Cowling[27] suggest that businesses rapidly outgrow the founder's capabilities—usually when the company reaches the ten-employee level or around $1 million in annual revenues. Adequate training and team building, where complementary skills are added to the company's management level, may mitigate the problem.

It is important to distinguish between two kinds of owners (or managers) of SMEs who, as L. Fillion[28] has observed, behave quite differently: "the entrepreneur and the operator. In the first type, vision and animation of the workforce are prevailing elements of management; in the second, planning, allocation, and verification are the paramount elements of the style. But in both cases performance can be improved by training, which should be seen as an ongoing process."

Access to New Technology

Access to new technology can be a problem, too—at least for the more sophisticated companies that depend on inside and also outside sources of technology. But in his book *Innovation and Entrepreneurship*,[29] Peter Drucker contends that high technology is not the only (or even the most important) source of new enterprises. Economic development and new jobs are being generated by a new entrepreneurial management culture that is being applied not in high-tech companies (where mismanagement is common) only but in new sectors of the economy—such as municipal services, health care, and education—that could be described as medium, low, or even no tech. Although access to technology might be a problem in some cases, don't feel discouraged about going global just because your business is not regarded as high tech.

All these factors are discussed in more detail in chapter 4, with specific references to the obstacles that may hinder the development of international e-commerce for SMEs.

The International Market

Globalization is transforming the environment in which small companies operate. As with all major changes, globalization brings both opportunities and risks. Small companies are now able to tackle local and international markets. This means that small companies in other parts of the world may take an interest in the market that your small company now serves and that you thought was free from international competition. Directly or through partnerships with other small companies in other parts of the world, whether using electronic commerce tools or not, small companies are going global. The trend began before the introduction of the Internet. The new technologies are likely to accelerate it.

Export activities tend to promote growth, increase profits, and transform companies into more sophisticated players in their own markets. According to the SBA,[30] companies engaged in international trade are 20 percent more productive and 9 percent more likely to stay financially solvent than nonexporters. In many cases, the various demands of the international market add flexibility to a company's culture; this characteristic may, in turn, be useful in introducing additional, perhaps more customized products and services to the local market as well.

Exporting is booming in the United States, and small businesses are beginning to realize that the world might be their market. The number of small exporting businesses in the United States grew from 66,000 in 1987 to 202,000 in 1997 (see figure 1.1 below).[31] And the fastest growth has been in the very small business sector (businesses with fewer than twenty employees). Small businesses are responsible for 31 percent of all U.S. exports of merchandise, and this percentage is growing. There are no comparable statistics for the services sector, but it is generally believed that that percentage could be even higher. As elements of the world economy become more interdependent, export opportunities for small businesses become more important—and, in some cases, imperative—for survival.

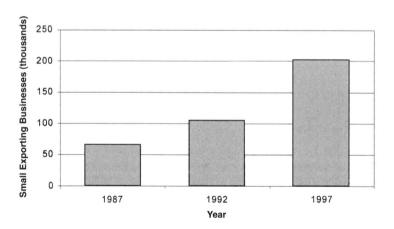

Figure 1.1
Number of Small Exporting Businesses in the United States (thousands)
Source: U.S. Small Business Association (1999).[14]

The added benefits of the export business translate into better working conditions for employees: American workers producing for export earn 15 percent more and get 11 percent higher employment benefits than nonexport workers.

We have already established that small companies generate jobs and spur economic development. But among small companies, those capable of the greatest growth are the ones that target the international market. The quest to gain and maintain international competitiveness is important for success in the international market and also in regional markets, since competition in those markets will come, sooner or later, from foreign companies.

Several countries have established public policies directed toward small exporting companies, such as the *consorzi esportazione* in Italy, the SOFTEX (Export Software) Program in Brazil, and the Northern Development Company in the United Kingdom.[32] Stated simply, that policy is that companies that aspire to international competitiveness should be the focus of policy.[33]

Business-to-business e-commerce is likely to constitute the major portion of international e-commerce. For that reason small-company owners should pay special attention to opportunities that might exist or that they might create themselves to enter this sector in their respective supply chains.

In targeting countries for exports, consider the kinds of products and services that your company offers. Rather than exporting to developed countries only, your best opportunities may lie elsewhere. The big five developing countries mentioned above, for example, could double their trade in the next twenty years, projecting current trends. Smaller countries also may be (or may become) a good target importer for your business. Think of the whole world as your target market, and then select your best opportunities.

Special Projects and Programs for SMEs

The very popular play (also a movie) *Fiddler on the Roof* tells the story of a Jewish village in nineteenth-century Russia that is frequently rampaged by the Cossacks. On one of these occasions when the village is under attack once again, the main character Tevye raises his hands to the sky and talks to God in despair: "We have been the chosen people for two thousand years. Isn't it time You choose someone else?"

Small companies tend to be the priority of governments all over the world, as well—the "chosen" people. Owners of SMEs all over the world probably feel increasingly like Tevye—jaded about the array of projects and programs in support of small business that governments propose and that seldom materialize into anything useful. These proposals are made for at least partly political reasons, of course: politicians try to exploit this large group of potential voters. But once you take away the empty promises, only a few programs actually help small companies and are worth investigating.

The Incubator

Incubators for emerging companies have been created all over the world. They are organizations set up by the state or by a university in which startup companies can install themselves in the early stages of their development and receive support in the form of lawyers, accountants, marketing specialists, and other services. The degrees of success of these arrangements vary, but most of them are little more than a space for lease under slightly better conditions than the overall market would allow, since a public organization is subsidizing the effort. Incubators tend to be diverse, nurturing any kind of new company. But the most successful ones tend to be those that concentrate in one particular sector of the economy, such as software or biotechnology, where the synergies between the companies themselves can be an opportunity for the individual development of each one.

Traditional incubators are organized as government entities or not-for-profit societies. A newer phenomenon is the company incubator, in which the organization is a for-profit company that offers many more services to the startup company and takes an equity stake in the company in return for these services. The new dot-com companies constitute one sector in which company incubators tend to specialize. The idea started in the United States with a company called IdeaLab and was then taken up by several other companies in the United States (e-hatchery, Divine

Interventures, and others) but also in other parts of the world, such as Gorillapark in Europe or i-cubo in Brazil.[34]

The Consortium of Export Companies

An interesting type of organization has developed in Italy: a small number of SMEs (fifteen to twenty-five), generally from the same sector, jointly form *consorzi*, nongovernment organizations (NGOs) to promote their exports. The *consorzi* promote training, improve product quality, invest in expensive machinery to be shared, organize trade missions to other countries, participate in trade shows all over the world, and contract export services such as customs clearances, translation, and transport.[35] The Italian government invests annually in these organizations to help promote the country's exports. There are around 600 *consorzi* in Italy, involving 20,000 companies. They are responsible for a significant portion of the country's total exports. Many other countries and regions in Europe and other parts of the world are now following this example.

Training

The U.S. SBA has instituted many programs to help small companies, ranging from training, financing, and information to active support for exports.[36] An initiative by the Group of Eight (G-8) (see Chapter 4) launched a project called G-8 Global Marketplace for SMEs, which helped to raise awareness about the importance of globalization for small companies from different parts of the world (within and outside of the G-8). The project also contributed to the regulatory aspect of international e-commerce and fostered the development of a wide range of test beds for demonstration of the possibilities and hurdles for the implementation of e-commerce.[37]

Without sufficient data to demonstrate it, I would like to advance the idea that perhaps the best government initiative to foster the birth and development of new companies is to support or even mandate the offering of entrepreneurial courses at all training levels (see Entrepreneurship, above). Education may encourage hidden entrepreneurial talents and ideas to emerge and new ones to develop. All the rest is consequential.

Trends

SMEs are appearing everywhere, and their combined share of the economy is growing. Their rates of development and success will depend on the specific conditions in the countries where they try to do business.

Since SMEs are generating new jobs, their importance to the economy is critical—particularly for countries with growing populations. The share of women employees and managers is higher in smaller enterprises, workers are younger than average, and their level of education is lower than that of workers in larger enterprises. Governments in general should be aware of this social dimension to job creation: SMEs favor heterogeneity and diversity.

When a student graduates from college, some Latin languages call the graduation ceremony *formatura*, meaning that he or she is "formed." It conveys the idea that they are ready for the market, as if what they learned in those few years would be applicable and valid forever. American universities, on the other hand, call that ceremony *commencement*. By chance or wisdom, they are exactly right: today, when students graduate, they are ready to commence their working lives, and learning is a major part of that process.

The computer debuted in the SME as a tool for the owner's assistant, who used it to type memos and letters, send and receive faxes, and create tables and charts. Then the Internet emerged as the toy and homework aid for the owner's children at home. Eventually came e-commerce and e-business. Suddenly the SME owner's very business is at stake. Almost overnight, the office assistant's tool and the children's toy became a threat to the business. So now SME owners are paying more attention to the Internet. The trend is irreversible: computers and devices connected to the Internet will be part of every business within the next few years. The new generation coming up will effect the transition effortlessly, since they are already used to electronic gadgets. But the existing pool of managers will have to be trained and become aware of the trend. Without much exaggeration, the cost of hiding one's head in the sand could be the business itself.

Small companies in the Internet business raised huge sums of money from venture capitalists in the United States. That phenomenon led many people to the false conclusion that capital is now available to SMEs. But it is still difficult to raise capital, and the process is cumbersome. Innovative schemes have been suggested and sometimes implemented. Dr. Mohammed Yunus, an economics professor in Bangladesh, came up with the concept of a "village bank," where very small amounts of capital are loaned to poor individuals to start a microbusiness within a supportive and disciplined peer group. The idea was transformed into a profitable bank[38] that has 2 million borrowers. The default rate is less than 2 percent, owing to a simple control mechanism: if a borrower defaults, his or her community is blocked from additional credit. So the communities themselves ensure that the payments are made. The idea was a success in Bangladesh and was later transferred to Latin America by Accion International[39] and also to inner cities in the United States. More of these innovations are likely to be developed and can fundamentally change the landscape of opportunities for many people all over the world.

The direct use of e-commerce for international trade is still small so far, for three reasons:

• Access to the Internet is uneven worldwide, limiting the number of buyers who are interested in international purchases.

• The high concentration of e-commerce initially in the United States, mostly for internal trade, dwarfs the percentage of e-commerce for international trade.

• Concerns and difficulties associated with payment and delivery services for international transactions persist.

But these factors are already changing quickly. As will be shown in the next chapters, a new opportunity is here for those with the drive to take it. In the frank words of Andrew Grove, chairman of Intel and futuristic guru, "In the future, all companies will be Internet companies or they will not be companies at all." The good news for SMEs is that they now have a better chance to succeed, since they can obtain their inputs more cheaply and sell to a much wider market, including the international market. The bad news is that other SMEs that they have never heard of might be looking at their own markets.

In summary, opportunities are knocking at the doors of SMEs. But the technological changes are enormous and are affecting everyone. An apt metaphor regarding the impact of these changes is that of the tsunami— the gigantic wave that sometimes builds up in the Pacific. When you are in a boat and receive a tsunami warning, you can do one of three things:

• Wait for the wave to reach its peak and follow its course down naturally, going in whatever direction it takes you.

• Cut the wave top at a certain angle—a risky business, similar to spaceships navigating their return to the atmosphere.

• Dash off to a safe harbor if there is one within reach.

The only thing you cannot do is to ignore it and think, "Maybe it won't get me." The business revolution we are living through now is like a tsunami: you can let it carry you where it will, surf it strategically to your advantage, or take a different course, but be well aware of its coming. It is unavoidable.

Recommended Further Reading

Drucker, P. *Innovation and Entrepreneurship*. New York: Harper Business, 1985.

Kaplan, J. *Startup: A Silicon Valley Adventure*. New York: Penguin Books, 1994.

Gavron, R., et al. *The Entrepreneurial Society*. London: Institute for Public Policy Research, 1998.

2

The Information Industry and the Internet Economy

Have you ever received a fax in a beach where you have never been before? You will.
—The Blue Man Group

The Digital Revolution

In the 1967 film *The Graduate*, Benjamin Braddock (Dustin Hoffman), a confused, disillusioned college graduate who is uncertain about his future, receives one word of advice from a slightly inebriated family associate: "plastics." It was the hot technology of the day and a catchword for a generation of career seekers. If *The Graduate* were remade today, the catchword would be "digital."

Digital technology is changing everything—the way telephone calls are made, text messages are sent, newspapers are published, music is distributed, and meetings are organized. The digital age has overturned the economic verities of the industrial age that persisted for over 150 years. Some of the products of digital technology are visible and even commonplace—digital cameras, personal computers, digital TV. But most of the changes wrought by digital capabilities are invisible but sweeping. The reliability and fuel efficiency of automobiles has nearly doubled, thanks in large part to the hundreds of computers employed in newer models. Cellular phone rates dropped when new digital models vastly increased the capacity of any given bandwidth. Cable TV systems began to offer greater choice, owing to the capabilities of digital signals. Wal-Mart, the vast American chain retailer, kept its prices low with the help of systems linking store inventories and suppliers to headquarters.

Examples could fill this chapter. One amazing outcome of digital technology has been the uncanny ability of the U.S. economy, at least for an extended period in the latter half of the 1990s and into the twenty-first century, to confound the expectations of Keynesian economists.[1] For a period far longer than at any other time in modern history, Americans have benefited from nearly full employment, solid economic growth, and almost zero inflation.

Though a review of the digital world could dwell on the specific technologies—microprocessors, fiber optics, satellites, and mass storage devices, among others—the phenomenon can be reduced to two critical trends: Moore's law and Metcalf's law. These are not laws of nature but rather are observations that have been validated over decades.[2] The failure of planners and regulators to consider the implications of these two laws has been the single greatest reason for missed predictions about the implications of emerging technologies—and therefore missed opportunities in the marketplace.

Moore's Law
Every eighteenth months for the foreseeable future, chip density (and hence, computing power) will double, while cost will remain constant.

Moore's law may be the most salient point in understanding the development of information technology. In 1965, Gordon Moore, a founder of Intel, was preparing a speech. When he started to graph data about the growth in memory-chip performance, he noticed a striking trend: each new chip contained roughly twice as much capacity as its predecessor, and each chip was released eighteen to twenty-four months after the previous chip. If this trend continued, he reasoned, computing power would rise exponentially over relatively brief periods of time. And one consequence of these advancements would be declining costs.

Moore's observation described a trend that has been sustained for at least thirty-five years: the central processor's capacity doubles every eighteen months. It has been the basis for the performance forecasts of many insightful planners. In the twenty-six years between 1971 and 1997, the number of transistors on a chip increased more than 3,200 times, from 2,300 on the Intel 4004 microprocessor to 7.5 million on the Intel Pentium II processor.[3] Meanwhile, other components—mass storage, modems, CD-ROM drives, and even monitors—also increased capacity while keeping prices constant (or even lowering them). Between 1996 and 1998 alone, the retail cost of the personal computer fell nearly 23 percent annually.[4]

Metcalf's Law

Networks dramatically increase in value with each additional node or user. The value of utilizing a network is equal to the square of the number of other users utilizing it.

Robert Metcalf was the principal inventor of Ethernet (the famous protocol for local area networks), which he developed while working for Xerox. Metcalf's law is known to economists as the principle of network externalities, which refers to the increase in value to all users of a communications service as more users join the network. For example, when only a few businesses and households had telephones, they were of limited value, and there was limited incentive to subscribe. Likewise, in the early days of e-mail, systems were proprietary; large companies had their own internal e-mail systems that were not connected to the outside world. And online services, such as CompuServe and America Online, had e-mail systems that allowed exchange only with other members of that service. Subscribers of different services could not exchange e-mail with each other. So the operation of Metcalf's law can be a hindrance to technological development.

Fax machines existed for decades before their use became widespread in businesses as well as homes. The usefulness of a fax machine grows exponentially, up to a certain point, with the number of users. So only when fax machines reached a critical mass—aided by the decreasing costs described in Moore's law—did faxes "suddenly" become ubiquitous. As telephone service gradually passed 50 percent of household penetration in the United States (in 1946), enough people knew someone who had a phone to be encouraged to subscribe themselves. Likewise, when the Internet introduced the possibility of widespread e-mail for anyone, those who used proprietary e-mail systems could not communicate with people on the public Internet, so they opened themselves to the common protocols of Internet e-mail, contributing to the pervasiveness—and utility—of e-mail.

Digital versus Analog Technologies

Under Moore's law, any process that can be enhanced or created using silicon-based intelligence has been and will continue to get smaller, faster, cheaper, and better. Conversely, any process that depends on mechanical and physical means will see its costs increase in concert with energy, labor, and capital costs. For example, online information acquisition becomes cheaper as devices such as PCs decrease in cost and as network externalities broaden the market for such services. In contrast, the cost of information in the form of traditional books, newspapers, and magazines will continue to rise.

It is critical to be aware that many traditional businesses can create new opportunities and hold down costs by employing digital technologies. Indeed, much of the success of the American economy in the 1990s came about from this marriage of digital with analog. FedEx is in the business of moving millions of physical goods on trucks and planes every day. But by employing highly sophisticated digital technologies, the company has become increasingly efficient. FedEx has also at times gained market share by being able to offer customers enhancements such as tracking, online scheduling, and integrated manifest creation. Similar implementations can—and have—filled casebooks.

Characterizing the Information Industry

With the blurring of the boundaries of traditional information industries, it is necessary to be more precise in describing information businesses today. In particular, we must differentiate among content, process, and format.

Content is the information provided by its producer (for instance, an author or a news agency). Process refers to both the handling and the transmission of the content. And format is the way the content is made available to the user.

For example, thirty years ago, watching television meant using a particular format—pictures on the video tube—provided through virtually the only process available, on-air broadcasting. "Television" referred to the box as well as the technology that produced and transmitted the content. Today, television is far more complex. The content of picture and sound using the video format may be received by means of a variety of processes, including the old broadcast signal but now also encompassing identical content through coaxial cable, satellite signal, videocassette tape, optical disk, or even twisted-pair telephone lines.

Today the process determines how the medium is regulated. In particular, content that is broadcast has a different set of legal parameters than the identical content that is distributed by means of cable or other processes. In the United States, for example, a broadcast featuring political candidates is subject to equal-time provisions for other candidates. If a cable network carried the same show, it would be free of such provision. This difference is the result of old regulations that were put in place when television was, well, television.

Newspapers have historically been published on newsprint. Now newspaper publishers may provide information using a variety of processes and formats. The same content may be delivered through an online process accessed by the user through the Internet or a news service provided in batches to the user. Or it may come to the user by means of a satellite or a terrestrial wireless system, a circuit-switched telephony connection, or a packet-switched connection (going the last mile to the user by coaxial or fiber-optic cable).

From a user standpoint, some of these process distinctions are meaningful in terms of costs, performance, and availability. But generally the public cares little about technologies. They care not about the details of how a cable company provides data or how a telephone provider tweaks access ADSL (asymmetric digital subscriber loop) to provide broadband Internet but about the quality and price of the services offered. From an industry standpoint, however, the stakes can be very high indeed, with winners and losers of considerable revenues involved. From a public-policy standpoint, major issues are at stake in the areas of regulation, development, and societal goals, such as democratization of information, universal access, privacy, and national security.

Size and Landscape of the Information Industry

None of the many attempts to establish the boundaries of the information industry has been perfectly satisfying. Figure 2.1 might help

The Information Business

GOVT MAIL	MAILGRAM	INTERNATL TEL SVCS	VANs	BROADCAST NETWORKS	DATABASES AND	PROFESSIONAL SVCS
PARCEL SVCS	TELEX	LONG DIST TEL SVCS		BROADCAST STATIONS	VIDEOTEX	
COURIER SVCS	EMS	LOCAL TEL SVCS	DBS	CABLE NETWORKS	NEWS SVCS	
OTHER DELIVERY				CABLE OPERATORS		FINANCIAL SVCS
SVCS					TELETEXT	ADVERTISING SVCS

MULTIPOINT DISTRIBUTION SVCS

DIGITAL TERMINATION SVCS
MOBILE SVCS   FM SUBCARRIERS

PRINTING COS   PAGING SVCS   BILLING AND   TIME-SHARING   SERVICE BUREAUS
LIBRARIES   METERING SVCS   ON-LINE DIRECTORIES
                                   MULTIPLEXING SVCS
                                                                     SOFTWARE SVCS
RETAILERS   BULK TRANSMISSION SVCS
NEWSSTANDS   INDUSTRY NETWORKS   SYNDICATORS AND
                                                                     PROGRAM PACKAGERS
                       DEFENSE TELECOM SYSTEMS   LOOSE-LEAF SVCS

                   SECURITY SVCS

                       CSS SVCS

                              COMPUTERS

                       PABXs

                                                          SOFTWARE PACKAGES
           RADIOS
           TV SETS   TELEPHONE SWITCHING EQUIP   DIRECTORIES
PRINTING AND   TELEPHONES   MODEMS   NEWSPAPERS
  GRAPHICS EQUIP TERMINALS   NEWSLETTERS
COPIERS   PRINTERS   CONCENTRATORS
                FACSIMILE   MULTIPLEXERS   MAGAZINES
                ATMs
CASH REGISTERS POS EQUIP
                BROADCAST AND   SHOPPERS
INSTRUMENTS   TRANSMISSION EQUIP
TYPEWRITERS   WORD PROCESSORS   AUDIO RECORDS
DICTATION EQUIP VIDEO TAPE RECORDERS   AND TAPES
BLANK TAPE   PHONOS, VIDEO DISC PLAYERS
  AND FILM   FILMS AND
                                                                          VIDEO PROGRAMS
                CALCULATORS

FILE CABINETS   MICROFILM , MICROFICHE
PAPER   BUSINESS FORMS   GREETING CARDS   BOOKS

SERVICES / PRODUCTS (vertical axis)
FORM ◄———————————— SUBSTANCE ►

ATM = Automatic teller machine   DBS = Direct broadcast satellite   POS = Point-of-sale
COS = Companies   EMS = Electronic message service   SVCS = Services
CSS = Carrier "smart" switch   PABX = Private automatic branch exchange   VAN = Value-added network

© 1995 President and Fellows of Harvard College, Program on Information Resources Policy.

Figure 2.1
Value Added in the Information Industry
Source: Benjamin M. Compaine and William H. Read, eds., *The Information Resources Policy Handbook* (Cambridge, Mass.: MIT Press 1999).

in understanding the situation. It shows most of the items associated with the information industry spread over the product-service and form-substance domains. The vertical axis ranges from products in the lower end to services in the upper end. The product and service distinction is common to both business practice and academic economics. At one pole, the idea of service connotes the consumer's continuing interaction with or dependence on the provider of the service or product. At the other extreme, a product in its purest form implies no interaction between supplier and consumer once an item has been bought. Moving from left to right on the map is a continuum of increased value added. This horizontal axis draws on the ideas of format, process, and substance. Format and process combined as form define the left-hand part of the horizontal axis. The right-hand part is pure substance.

It might seem obvious that computers, telecommunications, the media, and anything else tied to the Internet constitute the information industry. And generally that is true. Yet Dell, IBM, Apple, and Cisco, among many others, derive most of their income from manufacturing. They make information-related equipment, but they run factories and build products. The telephone companies, similarly, are among the largest owners of trucks and dispatching operations. Newspaper publishers are classified as manufacturers because their physical product emerges from huge presses with gears and motors that harken back to the height of the industrial revolution.

On the other hand, industries that are not usually considered to be part of the information industry may in fact be highly information intensive. Commercial airlines, for example, depend greatly on weather information, radar, computer-generated flight plans, and the autopilot that controls a large part of each plane's flight. So the boundaries are not clear-cut.

One possible definition of the information industry could include only those companies making revenues from actually selling information—including the media and excluding the manufacturers of equipment. But should banks and law firms, management consultants and accountants be included? They sell information. Some compilations have indeed calculated how large the information industry would be if these businesses were added to those that have traditionally been included.

The bottom line is that there is no ideal and practical schema for drawing neat boundaries around the businesses we could easily recognize as belonging in the information industry. Table 2.1 offers one take on the information industry. It incorporates most of the industries, whether manufacturing or services, that derive most of their revenue from retailing information or information-related infrastructure. The bottom line of the table adds other professional services that are information intensive. Under either configuration

Table 2.1
Information Industries and Gross Domestic Product, 1987 to 1995 (billions)

	1987	1988	1989
Communication services	$131	$136	$143
Entertainment services (visual and audio)	37	64	75
Equipment (hardware and software)	98	103	106
Professional information services	9	65	69
Publishing and printing	118	124	132
Total	$393	$492	$525
GDP	$4,692	$5,049	$5,438
Information industries as percent of GDP	8.4%	9.7%	9.7%
Other information intensive professional services[a]	N/A	$224	$250

Source: Program on Information Resources Policy, Harvard University (1996).[2]

the industry is substantial and, not surprisingly, growing faster than the overall economy—despite consistently falling prices in many segments.

In general, the information industry can be thought of as those industries in figure 2.1 and table 2.1, recognizing that sizable information components may exist in other arenas. The key distinction is between companies that sell mainly information or the processes for moving information and companies that sell other goods or services that have information consumption as part of their internal operations but not as their primary revenue stream.

Meanwhile, some of the greatest business uncertainties about Internet winners and losers have to do with the formats that will prevail—the old and new information processes. Paper, that venerable format, is being challenged by electronic representations on screens of various sizes and shapes. Newspaper, magazine, and book publishers need to be concerned with the rate of migration of their content to new formats. For example, as of 2000 there was little evidence that the slow erosion of newspaper circulation has been affected by the free and widespread availability of most newspaper content online. But publishers are concerned. Similarly,

Table 2.1
(*continued*)

1990	1991	1992	1993	1994	1995
$147	$153	$161	$171	$187	$205
81	83	89	94	103	109
129	129	141	126	168	196
129	137	147	158	172	194
136	137	144	151	155	165
$622	$639	$682	$700	$785	$869
$5,743	$5,916	$6,224	$6,553	$6,935	$7,253
10.8%	10.8%	11.0%	11.1%	10.7%	12.0%
$258	$278	$309	$336	$352	$403

the recorded music business is torn between the cheap cost of distributing its music to customers over the Internet and the readiness with which that digitized information may be easily copied and illegally distributed everywhere.

These concerns are well founded. The economics of distributing information created for the Internet is very different from the economics of distributing information that has been processed in a tangible format. The production of newspapers, encyclopedias, and the like is a manufacturing process. The outcome is traditional manufactured goods. The sale of one more newspaper incurs costs for paper, ink, and distribution that are usually greater than the circulation revenue that one newspaper brings in. Information distributed over the Internet, however, has the characteristics of what economics call a *public good*—that is, almost no marginal cost is incurred when additional units are produced. The cost of one more user accessing a newspaper publisher's Web site is close to zero. That's a great attraction—if distributors can derive enough revenue (so far usually from advertisers) to cover the fixed costs of gathering, processing, and storing the information that goes into their databases.

In 1999, Daimler Benz used as the tag line for its Dodge line of cars: "This changes everything." Whether it was an appropriate motto for their cars or not, it certainly *is* an appropriate tag line for the Internet.

The Internet

The Internet has been around for four decades, but most of that time for only academic use. It was only after www protocols were established in 1995 and the first browser (called Mosaic) was introduced in the same year that the juggernaut was set in motion. The widespread use of the Internet that emerged in the second half of the 1990s is a phenomenon that can only be described in orders of magnitude of change:

· In 1995, an estimated 18 million Americans were online. By February 1998, that number was up 244 percent to 62 million. By 2000, well over 100 million Americans (about half of the adult U.S. population)—137 million including Canadians—were online.[5]

· Advertising on the Internet, barely visible in 1996 at $267 million, more than tripled to $907 million in 1997 and had reached $3 billion in 1999.[6]

· Information sent over the Internet (traffic) was doubling every 100 days as *far back* as 1998.[7]

· At the end of 1996, about 627,000 Internet domain names had been registered. A year later the number of domain names had reached 1.5 million.[8]

· In 1996, Amazon.com, an Internet bookseller, recorded sales of less than $16 million. It sold $1.6 billion in merchandise (mostly books and CDs) in 1999.[9]

· In January 1997, Dell Computers recorded less than $1 million in computer sales per day on the Internet. The company reported reaching daily sales of $40 million less than three years later.[10]

· At the start of 1994, there were twenty newspapers worldwide with online editions. In mid-1998, there were 4,929. About half of these were outside the United States.[11]

• In the early 1990s, there were about 15 million e-mail accounts world-wide. In 2000, there were roughly 569 million e-mail accounts, with 333 million accounts in the United States alone.[12]

With this kind of evolution—*revolution* may be the more appropriate term—the Internet may be very different even in two or three years after the publication of this book. (That is why we are keeping current an online version of chapter 7 of this book; see chapter 7.) The Internet and its components are in such nascent form that the players and their positions in the industry are likely to change over very short periods. But the nature of the technologies behind the Internet does suggest several general positions that are likely to remain true:

• The Internet itself is not and is not likely to be "owned" by anyone or even a small group of companies.

• The business models for establishing revenue streams for Internet companies and for transforming Internet ventures into sound business propositions are not well developed today.

• In the foreseeable future, few ventures on the Internet are likely to kill off major segments of existing commerce. The Internet will expand choices and options. It will provide new competition for incumbent players, and unprepared companies may indeed disappear. But most will have abundant time to adapt to the Internet, either by using it to improve existing operations or by migrating to new platforms as both the technologies and audiences allow—assuming they are aware of and respond to these powerful changes.

Who Owns the Internet?
There was a joke of sorts making the rounds in 1998 that Bill Gates, the cofounder of Microsoft and at the time reportedly the richest man in the world, tried to buy the Internet. But he couldn't find out whose name should be on the check . . .

Indeed, unlike older business models based on proprietary systems and tangible assets, the Internet is a collection of technologies, hardware, software, and systems that does not lend itself to control.

There are many places to learn about the history and architecture of the Internet and the development of the World Wide Web.[13] The very short story is that the U.S. Defense Department's Advanced Research Project Agency (ARPA) initiated the ARPANET as a tool for linking academics doing defense and security work with military contractors. It was critical to create a network that had redundant communications paths so that even a natural disaster or a nuclear attack at one or several links would not bring down the system.

Moreover, the initial Internet was designed to use much of the existing telecommunications infrastructure. And lastly, it adopted the transmission control protocol/Internet protocol (TCP/IP), a standard set of rules that allows computers on different networks to communicate with one another. This was a public-domain protocol that worked across various proprietary computer operating systems and platforms.

There are, to be sure, some major players. But to best understand their role, it is first necessary to explain some of the key components of the Internet.

Telecommunications: Backbone and Retail Points of Presence

The bits that compose the text, sound, and pictures that traverse the globe are carried over a telecommunications platform that is much like—and in places is congruent with—the traditional telephone network. The connection between the user premises and the first network node is called "the last mile." Since most users access the Internet through the old telephone network, for them the last mile is the twisted-pair wire that links the user to the first central exchange.

Through this connection, users from homes and small offices have dialed up to call into Internet service providers (ISPs) who connect them to the Internet "backbone" providers. These latter have the high-bandwidth facilities that merge the data packets from many users to and from the servers around the world. Large businesses and institutions may have higher-speed connections to ISPs or even into the backbone directly. Through these connections, the user reaches an Internet point of presence (POP). POPs are the nodes to which users connect to gain access to the Internet. When consumers have their modems dial a phone number and "log on," they are dialing into a POP. A corporate network may have a high-speed line, such as a 1.5 Mb/s (Megabits per second), known as T-1, connected to a POP as well.

The backbones may be congested for several reasons, totally out of the user's control, depending on the time of day, special events, holidays, circuit breakdowns, and other conditions. The overall performance of your Internet connection depends on the speed of your last-mile connection, the speed of your ISP, and the state of the backbone at that particular time.

Layers of the Internet Economy

Although the physical aspects of any economy are still based on manufactured goods, the Internet economy is fundamentally different. This economy relies on high-speed Internet networks and Internet applications—new competitive tools for business and electronic intermediaries to increase the efficiency of Internet-driven markets.

A study by the Center for Research in Electronic Commerce (CREC) at the University of Texas created the following description of the Internet economy.[14] It differs somewhat in how it attributes revenues to the Internet sectors compared with the methods used for the information industry compilation in table 2.1.

CREC defines the Internet economy as being made up of companies directly generating all or part of their revenues from Internet or Internet-related products and services. These companies are the Internet infrastructure and Internet applications players, such as 3Com, Cisco, Dell, IBM, HP, Oracle, Microsoft, and Sun, whose products and services make it feasible to use the Internet for electronic commerce. For example, IBM sells servers and PCs that are used to gain access to the Internet. Similarly, 3Com sells modems, and Cisco sells routers, all used to gain access to the Internet. The Internet-related revenues from these companies, for example, are included in the estimates for the entire Internet economy.

Then there are companies that sell products and services over the Internet, including pure Internet-based sellers such as Amazon.com and eToys.com as well as bricks-and-mortar companies, such as L. L. Bean and Alaska Airlines, which are also conducting part of their business on the Internet. Further, electronic intermediaries or Internet middlemen, such as eBay or Etrade, act as catalysts by facilitating the interaction between buyers and sellers. So the overall Internet economy is made up of the revenues of infrastructure and applications players, electronic intermediaries, and online sellers.

The Internet economy is not just a collection of high-tech companies. It includes any company that generates revenues from the Internet. For example, a part of the revenues generated by traditional telecommunications companies are counted in this economy since they carry Internet protocol (IP) traffic over their miles and miles of copper, coaxial, and fiber-optic lines. The CREC study did not, however, count all revenues from all technology companies. Not even Cisco's revenues were considered to be 100 percent part of the Internet economy, since not all networking devices are attached to the Internet.

The CREC model divides the Internet economy into four sectors or layers: infrastructure, applications, intermediaries, and commerce.

Layer One: Infrastructure
The infrastructure layer includes companies with products and services that help create an IP-based network infrastructure. This infrastructure layer includes

- Internet backbone providers (e.g., Qwest, Worldcom),
- Internet service providers (e.g., MSN, AOL, Earthlink),
- Networking hardware and software companies (e.g., Cisco, Lucent, 3Com),
- PC and server manufacturers (e.g., Dell, Compaq, IBM),
- Security vendors (e.g., Axent, Checkpoint, Network Associates),
- Fiber-optics makers (e.g., Corning), and
- Line acceleration hardware manufacturers (e.g., Ciena, Tellabs, Pairgain).

Layer Two: Applications
Products and services in the applications layer build on the IP network infrastructure. This layer includes

• Internet consultants (e.g., USWeb/CKS, Scient),

• Internet commerce applications (e.g., Netscape, Microsoft, Sun, IBM),

• Multimedia applications (e.g., RealNetworks, Macromedia),

• Web development software (e.g., Adobe, NetObjects, Allaire, Vignette),

• Search-engine software (e.g., Inktomi, Verity),

• Online training (e.g., Sylvan Prometric, Assymetrix), and

• Web-enabled databases (only Internet- and intranet-related revenues are counted) (e.g., Oracle, IBM DB2, Microsoft SQL Server).

Layer Three: Intermediaries

Internet intermediaries increase the efficiency of electronic markets by facilitating the meeting and interaction of buyers and sellers over the Internet. They act as catalysts in the process through which investments in the infrastructure and applications layers are transformed into business transactions. This layer includes

• Market makers in vertical industries (e.g., VerticalNet, PCOrder),

• Online travel agents (e.g., Travelocity.com, Expedia.com),

• Internet ad brokers (e.g., Doubleclick, 24/7 Media),

• Online advertising (e.g., Yahoo!, ESPNSportszone),

• Online brokerages (e.g., ETrade, AmeriTrade, DLJDirect),

• Content aggregators (e.g., CNET, ZDNET, Broadcast.com), and

• Portals/content providers (e.g., Yahoo!, Excite, Lycos).

Layer Four: Commerce

Internet commerce involves the sales of products and services to consumers or businesses over the Internet. This layer includes

• E-tailers (e.g., Amazon.com, eToys.com),

• Manufacturers selling online (e.g., Cisco, Dell, IBM),

• Fee- or subscription-based companies (e.g., Hoovers Online.com, WSJ.com),

• Airlines selling online tickets, and

• Online entertainment and professional services.

Although many players are focused on one of these four levels, many others offer products or services across several. For instance, Microsoft and IBM are prominent players at the Internet infrastructure, applications, and Internet commerce layers, whereas AOL, with its acquisition of Netscape and Time Warner, became a key player in all layers.

Even though the four-layer Internet economy framework makes it difficult to separate revenues for multilayer players, the framework presents a more real-world view of the Internet economy landscape versus a single-layered measurement process. Further, the multilayered approach facilitates analysis of how companies choose to enter one Internet layer and choose later to extend their activities to the other Internet layers.

Basic Internet Statistics

Number of Users

How many Internet users are out there today? Account names are not good indicators, since many people have more than one account. The number of Internet hosts can be measured, but how many users do they serve? In fact, how do we characterize someone as a user—someone who uses it daily, at least once a week? Depending on the method used to produce the estimate, the numbers can vary widely. For the purposes of this book, we need only to establish that the number is very large, which is indisputable. Additionally, the adoption rate of the Internet around the world is simply unparalleled among technologies. It is being embraced much more rapidly than the telephone, radio, or TV (see figure 2.2).

The evolution has been extraordinary. Take the Activmedia measure,[15] produced in 1998. In 1997, 48 million people in the United States and 77 million worldwide had Internet access. From there on, the numbers grew very rapidly, leading to the projection of 207 million users in the United States and more than 720 million worldwide in 2005.[16] As the rest of the world wakened to the Internet revolution, the percentage of U.S. users in relation to the world total has begun to

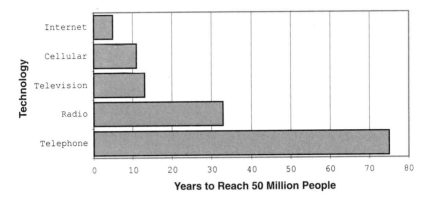

Figure 2.2
Adoption Rate for Major Technologies
Source: World Trade Organization (1998).[15]

decrease. In fact, in 1999 the rest of the world caught up with the United States in terms of Internet usage: in that year, about 50 percent of all users were in the United States, and 50 percent were elsewhere.[17] The number of worldwide users today and projected for 2005 is shown in figure 2.3.

A study by the consulting company Ernst & Young[18] showed that 41 percent of U.S. households have at least one PC and that half of them are online. The trend toward connecting existing and new PCs to the network is strong: not only are new PCs sold connection-ready, but access to the Internet is one of the primary reasons for purchases of new or replacement PCs. This trend can also be verified internationally. Table 2.2 shows that information technology has been growing rapidly and that two-thirds of all the PCs in use worldwide today have Internet access. Access takes many different forms, but counting only fixed-line and wireless telephone lines, there should be 1.4 billion lines worldwide in 2001.[19] This figure shows that there is still a lot of room for growth once other appliances, such as personal digital assistants (PDAs) and cellular phones, also become access points to the Internet. Lucent's Bell Laboratories predicts that by 2006 there will be 6 billion units connected to the Internet, equivalent to the world's population today.[20]

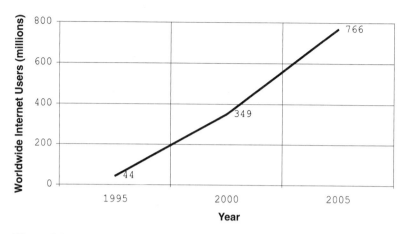

Figure 2.3
Worldwide Intenet Users (in millions)
Source: *Computer Industry Almanac* (1999).[16]

Table 2.2
The World Gets Connected (millions)

Category	1991	1996	2001
Fixed-line telephone lines	545	741	1,000
Wireless telephone lines	16	135	400
PC	123	245	450
Internet hosts	<1	16	110
PCs with Internet connections	4	60	300

Source: International Telecommunications Union (1998).[19]

The User Profile

The average user of the Internet is a thirty-three-year-old married white male who speaks English as a first language and makes over $50,000 a year. Table 2.3 depicts the user profile in more detail.

Size of the Network

As with everything else related to the Internet, growth rates are striking. For instance, registering the first million domain names took four years; increasing from 4 million to 5 million domain names took three months.[21]

Table 2.3
Internet User Profile: Average Age, 33 years

	Percent
Gender:	
Male	65
Female	35
Yearly income:	
Over $50,000	44
$30,000–$40,000	10
$40,000–$50,000	31
$10,000–$30,000	12
Under $10,000	3
Marital Status:	
Married	46
Single	31
Other	23
Other:	
College or university degree	57
White	87
English as first language	90
Internet access from home	55

Source: http://www.mysite.com (2000).

The telecommunications side of the Internet is highly competitive at all levels. At the end of 1999, there were 5,078 ISPs in the United States, up 233 from a year earlier. These were the "on ramps" to the Internet. Among these, 184 were considered national ISPs by virtue of having a presence in more than twenty-five area codes.[22] By the spring of 1998— barely four years after Netscape introduced the Web to the mass audience—92 percent of the U.S. population lived in counties with more than three competing ISPs, up from 75 percent the previous year. Dramatic growth was recorded in other parts of the world as well.

Measuring the Internet Economy
Using the CREC model, the Internet economy generated an estimated $301 billion in revenues in the United States and was responsible for 1.2 million jobs in 1998.

Table 2.4
Measuring the Internet Economy: U.S. Revenues and Jobs, 1998

	Estimated Internet Revenues (billions)	Attributed Internet Jobs
Internet infrastructure layer	$115	372,462
Application infrastructure layers	56	230,629
Intermediary/market maker layer	58	252,473
Internet commerce layer	102	481,990
Total Internet economy[a]	$301	1,203,799

Source: Center for Research in Electronic Commerce (1998).[23]
a. Total subtracts an estimate $30 billion in double-counted revenue and jobs between commerce and other layers.

Revenues and jobs were measured using the four-layer structure and are shown in table 2.4. The component indicators in each level were added, with some adjustment, to make up the larger revenues indicator and jobs indicator.[23]

The Internet economy already rivals the size of century-old sectors, such as energy ($223 billion), automobiles ($350 billion), and telecommunications ($270 billion). The average revenue generated per Internet-economy worker is about $250,000, or about 65 percent higher than a worker from an industrial-economy counterpart.[24]

SMEs in the Internet Economy

In the bricks-and-mortar world, when smaller retailers hear that a Wal-Mart is coming into their territory, they often fear for their existence. When a major airline decides to fly routes that had been the province of a small local carrier, the small airline may have similar concerns for the future. In the old economy, it was realistic to fear that the big guys would eat the lunch of the small ones if they went head to head.

But the virtual world is subject to different truths. Certainly the big boys—whether new and flush with venture capital or old and just flush—have some advantages. However, the Internet levels the playing field. It is a system that can be used to a smaller player's advantage as easily as to a larger player's. Here's why.

The cost of the infrastructure is spread across millions of users, which is more of a strategic advantage to the smaller players than to the larger ones. Consider this example: to start a traditional daily newspaper, one had to buy a multimillion-dollar printing press. Starting a Web site to provide similar content requires leasing a hosting service for a few hundred dollars monthly.

The Internet expands the universe of sellers. The big guys can do more marketing. But the smaller players can economically reach national and international customers that had never before been on their radar. As marginal revenue, any such additional customers may be quite profitable.

The Internet expands the universe of suppliers as well. Whether for raw materials for a homebuilder or printed letterhead for an accounting firm, having access to information about a wider range of suppliers can save substantial costs.

Beyond just expanding a customer base, the Internet allows suppliers to offer new kinds of services and provides new opportunities for new forms of business. For example, one firm that had been selling an enterprise software system had required an engineer to go onsite to install the system. Technical support was an expensive and ongoing concern. Using an application service provider (ASP)[25] Internet model, the company created a functionally equivalent system that resided on the software company's own host, reducing installation and support costs. It allowed the firm to offer a free, "lite" version of the service, which could also be used as a new marketing tool.

The technologies known collectively as the Internet can be viewed as raising obstacles to incumbents or creating opportunities for them. Those who simply try to protect their turf may have some short-term successes. But those who recognize the new opportunities and embrace the Internet's growing possibilities will not only survive but thrive in the next decade and beyond.

Financial Markets and the New Economy

At the start of 2000, Pittsburgh-based U.S. Steel, the industrial giant assembled by J. P. Morgan in 1901, had a market capitalization (price of its stock times total number of shares) of $2.7 billion. It had revenues in 1999 of about $5.2 billion.

FreeMarkets, a Pittsburgh-based Internet-based company founded in 1995 to help companies like U.S. Steel buy supplies, had a market capitalization nearly four times as great—and revenues of about $15 million, 0.3 percent that of U.S. Steel. Five months later, FreeMarket's market capitalization plunged 80 percent, but it was still worth half of U.S. Steel.

• Why does Microsoft earn $8 billion on $21 billion in sales while AT&T earns $5.2 billion on $60 billion of revenue?

• How can a new company with under $5 billion in annual revenue (America Online) negotiate a merger with an old media company with $17 billion in revenue (Time Warner) and yet own 55 percent of the combined entity?

• How can a couple of recent college graduates raise $10 million for a startup venture based on ten PowerPoint slides flashed before a room full of hard-nosed venture-capital investors?

These are some of the questions that were being asked as the high-tech economy took off at the end of the twentieth century. Answers are both refreshingly straightforward and infuriatingly complex.

That many of the so-called new economy ventures are highly valued despite low revenue and little or no profitability is not startling. Investment is about the future. A new, small enterprise with a sound business model may be expected to grow faster than a mature firm in a mature industry (think tires, newspapers, steel). Investors are buying the future. The dot-com companies, along with many of those enterprises that are expected to grow with the Internet, make logical choices for investing.

In May 2000, approximately 430 nontech stocks were listed in the Standard & Poor Index (S&P) of 500 publicly traded companies in the New York Stock Exchange. They were selling (based on the actual share price) for about seventeen times projected 2000 earnings (price-over-earnings ratio, P/E), close to the S&P's index historic average. The remaining seventy tech stocks in the S&P were selling at about forty times their 2000 projected earnings, which seems very high. But many economists did not find that far-fetched. As explained by the chief economist and global investment strategist for Deutsche Bank Securities, "The outstanding growth prospects for this group—my conservative forecast calls for five-year annual earnings growth of about 25 percent—means that the investor at these P/E levels is paying only 1.7 times the growth rate. Some might find this a little rich, but I don't think so, given technology's bright global prospects and decreasing cyclicality."[26]

One theory supporting higher valuations in the new economy incorporates the value of network externalities to help explain future growth. That is, as more personal computers, personal digital assistants, cell phones, wireless appliances, servers, printers, and faxes are shipped to customers, the more valuable the total network becomes to everyone. This multiplies the effects of the monetary value of these devices and the infrastructure that supports them, feeding the growth beyond the metrics used in the old economy.

Plenty of venture capital has been available to promote cutting-edge-technology Internet ventures. In 1999, venture-capital investments totaled nearly $36 billion, up 150 percent from the previous year.[27] The down side of all this capital being thrown at numerous ventures is that many will not survive. Most at risk are e-commerce and content sites on the World Wide Web that have no bricks-and-mortar relatives. This holds true even when the venture is backed by a deep-pocket venture capitalist.

In this category, 2000 saw a shakeout of several high-profile startups of 1998 and 1999. ToySmart, an online toy store majority owned by the Walt Disney Co., was shuttered. Violet.com, a specialty retailer, burned through $13 million in several months before the funders pulled the plug. Boo.com, an online apparel retailer, spent most of its $135 million in capital provided by such big names as J. P. Morgan and the Bennetton family before it went into liquidation.[28]

New ventures based on manufacturing goods seem to have a greater success rate. The chief executive of Internet network-equipment leader Cisco Systems estimated there were 400 to 500 startups in his industry from 1999 through mid-2000. Many of them were being bought along the way by Cisco, Lucent, Nortel, and smaller players, usually for stock.[29]

The Internet has been the twenty-first-century equivalent of the California gold rush in the mid-nineteenth century, when a window of opportunity allowed small players to grow large and for the established players to expand and when few models were certain about work. While there is considerable certainty about the future of the Internet itself, there is also great uncertainty about many aspects of its economics and markets. The ups and downs of the valuation of Internet companies in large measure reflect this dichotomy: many investors and entrepreneurs do not want to miss the gold rush. But no one knows exactly the timing or formula for what will work and what will not. In short, investors are playing statistically. They buy a large number of different companies. One or two big winners may be enough to offset all eventual losses.

Recommended Further Reading

Davis, S., and C. Meyer. *BLUR: The Speed of Change in the Connected Economy.* New York: Warner Books, 1998.

Dertouzos, M. *What Will Be.* San Francisco: Harper, 1997.

Seybold, P. *Customers.com.* New York: Times Business, 1998.

3

Electronic Commerce: Opportunities in the International Market

Wouldn't it be plausible to launch a dollar.com site to sell $1 bills for 90 cents and make money out of banner ads?
—The Economist

Overview

The movement toward conducting commercial transactions online is steady and gaining momentum. It did not start with the Internet, though. It started with telephone orders for items advertised in catalogs and on television, mostly in the United States, and was accelerated by the advent of buying products and services by fax. More recently and much more intensely, the Internet has expanded the realm of online purchasing.

People are already using the Internet for many different steps in the transaction process—to search for specific products or for all the existing alternatives or offerings of a product, to check out different retailers for the best price, to buy goods and services, to ask for and receive technical support, and in some cases even to have the product delivered online.

This chapter outlines the different steps involved in an electronic transaction and explains how electronic commerce is being conducted in various regions and in different formats, emphasizing commerce conducted across national borders. The very term *cross-border* takes on a different meaning in the context of electronic commerce. When products or services are delivered online, where exactly are the borders? Imagine a painting executed by an artist in China, stored on a server in Singapore, sold electronically to a customer in Mexico who has his Internet account in the United States and pays by a credit card that was issued by a Spanish bank that has a branch at the corner of the customer's home street in Mexico. The electronic transaction is completed when a copy of the painting is printed on the customer's home printer. To which country's gross domestic product (GDP) should this transaction be credited? Who records the transaction, and how? Are any taxes due? To whom? Where? And in what currency?

One striking characteristic of electronic commerce through the Internet is that it is not simply business as usual with a slightly different twist. As pointed out by *Information Strategy,* "One of the most important characteristics of electronic commerce is that it rewrites the rules of selling, but not necessarily in the way you expect."[1] This revolution is different from the introduction of computers, machines that some people understood well and most people didn't. It is not a case of one party being more knowledgeable than another; it is a case in which everyone perceives that something big is taking shape but nobody knows exactly what it is or what form it will ultimately take.

Small to medium-size businesses still face many obstacles on the way to full participation in electronic commerce. Some are mentioned here, but they are presented more systematically in chapter 4.

Yet Another Set of Internet Statistics

Consumer Spending on the Net

Not all internet users are interested in buying, of course: e-mail and information search have been by far the main impetus behind the explosive growth in Internet use. According to the Angus Reid Group, 120 million people have already purchased goods or services over the Internet worldwide, and that number is growing rapidly.[2] IDC, another market-research company, counted more modest numbers—around 50 million people—as shown in Table 3.1, and predicted that Internet sales will double again in 2001 to $223 billion as it has done since 1998.[3]

In the United States alone, consumer Net purchases during the Christmas season of 1998 increased fourfold over 1997: from $1.3 billion to over $5 billion, according to the Marketing Corporation of America. These online Christmas sales in 1998 were nearly double the

Table 3.1
Growth of E-commerce

	1995	1996	1997	1998	1999	2000	2001
Web users (millions)	15.3	27.8	50.2	71.3	96.6	129.2	174.6
Web buyers (millions)	3.5	7.01	13.9	21.8	32.2	46.9	68.4
Web buyers per users	22.9%	25.2%	27.7%	30.6%	33.3%	36.3%	39.2%
Revenues (billions)	$0.3	$2.6	$10.6	$28.9	$65.5	$123.3	$223.1
Revenues per Web buyer	$86	$371	$763	$1,325	$2,034	$2,627	$3,262

Source: IDC (1999).[3]

Table 3.2
Internet Business-to-consumer Growth in the World (billions)

	1999	2003
eMarketer	$98	$1,244
Dataquest	$31	$380

Source: eMarketer and Dataquest (1999).[7]

initial predictions, amounting to roughly 3 percent of total retail sales. In 1999, 25 million people spent $7 billion on the holiday season. By 2003, according to Forrester Research, Internet sales should reach between 4 and 5 percent of total retail sales: 40 million households in the United States alone will spend over $100 billion through the Net.[4]

E-commerce numbers are difficult to compare since organizations' definitions of e-commerce and measurement methods vary. Table 3.2 gives an idea of the disparity between two companies' measurements of Internet business-to-consumer sales for the same year. One company projects 2003 sales of $380 billion, and the other estimates $1,244 billion. The difficulty stems from the lack of a clear definition of e-commerce terms and expressions. Transactions realized on auction sites, for instance, involve both business-to-consumer (B2C) and consumer-to-consumer (C2C) operations and are very difficult to account for.

Early Internet users were computer specialists, and thus until 1998 computer items were the best sellers. This has tended to change, however, as the Internet has become more mainstream. Table 3.3 shows the distribution of online sales of products and services in the United States in the first quarter of 2000. The best-selling item was travel, which sent computer items to second place, even if you add hardware and software items. Third and fourth places are held now by auctions (a separate item statistically but one that involves all the other items) and apparel. Then comes books, an early winner probably attributable to both the nature of the product and to the Amazon.com's initial success and media coverage.

Skeptics see the evolution of online commerce merely as a substitute for newspapers inserts and claim that shoppers tend to peruse the information on the Web and then buy in real stores.[5] Most critics, however,

Table 3.3
Goods and Services Purchased Online, First Quarter 2000

Good or Service	Amount (millions)	Percent
Travel	$2,000	32.9%
Computer hardware	852	14.0
Auctions	644	10.5
Apparel	619	10.1
Books	461	7.5
Music and video	340	5.6
Consumer electronics	287	4.7
Computer software	257	4.2
Flower, gifts, cards	195	3.2
Health and beauty	153	2.5
Toys	147	2.4
Home and garden	82	1.3
Sports equipment	69	1.1
Total	$6,106	100.0%

Source: Harris Interactive (2000).[5]

feel that as each new generation grows more familiar with computers, e-commerce will grow substantially.

Business-to-Business and Total Sales

Although consumer transactions are much more visible to the public, the business-to-business arena is where e-commerce will explode. A recent report projects that electronic business-to-business transactions will reach 53 percent of the total number of business transactions by the year 2004 in the United States, at the startling figure of $3 trillion.[6] The well-known semiconductor company Intel started business-to-business selling in July 1998 with the target of $1 billion for the year. The target was reached in only two weeks. It is now selling over $1 billion a month over the Net. How many companies will follow suit, and when?

And what is the figure for the market as a whole? As we have seen, estimates vary widely from $100 billion to several hundred billion dollars of revenues generated directly over the Net. The European Commission refers to some $200 billion in electronic commerce over the Internet in

Europe at this recent turn of the century, but it is difficult to determine what type of electronic commerce these numbers represent. For 2003, the eMarketer group predicts that total B2B sales in Europe will be $766 billion, while IDC predicts that they will be only $367 billion.[7] For 2005, the forecast done by the Gartner Group raises that number in Europe to $2.3 trillion. Table 3.4 shows the forecasts for 2005 from the Gartner Group for the major world markets. One interesting implication of these numbers is that Europe and Asia (Japan plus the other Asian countries) are closing the gap between them and the United States in terms of B2B e-commerce adoption.

As we have seen, total sales on the Internet are still difficult to measure today. Whatever the actual numbers turn out to be, the upward trend shows tremendous growth. Forrester Research, for instance, predicted in 1997 that business-to-business sales through the Web would reach $327 billion in 2002. In late 1998, that figure was revised to $842 billion. Some transactions are not recorded anywhere, leading to widely varying speculations about numbers. Projections for total sales (B2B plus B2C) are the sum of two estimates and are even more difficult to forecast. Activmedia, for instance, in a published survey, reports e-commerce revenues in 1998 as $74 billion (much larger than the numbers shown above) and predicts growth to $1.23 trillion by 2002.[8] Although very large, this number matches Gartner's projections in Table 3.4. As we move forward, more and more commercial transactions, both business-to-consumer and business-to-business, will be done electronically, and it seems reasonable to state that in the first few years of this century (by 2004 or 2005), e-commerce revenues will total $7 trillion, which is equivalent to the U.S. GDP today.[9]

Table 3.4
Business-to-Business E-Commerce Worldwide (billions)

	North America	Europe	Asia and Pacific Islands	Japan	Latin America	World
1999	$91.0	$31.8	$9.2	$11.0	$1.0	$145.0
2005	2,840	2,340	992.0	861.0	124.0	7.29

Source: Gartner Group (2000), <http://www4.gartner.com/init>, accessed March 2000.

How Are SMEs Responding to the Challenge?

Knowing that customers were at the other end of the computer line, companies started to build Web sites. But many built a Web presence more for institutional reasons (staying technologically current) than for actual business purposes. A Booz-Allen & Hamilton report shows that 92 percent of executives believe the Internet will reshape business strategy and the marketplace, but according to Prodigy Communications, only one-third of all small businesses in the United States are online.[10]

The auction sites are one area where SMEs have jumped into e-commerce activities. An estimated 600,000 SMEs were selling their products and services via auction e-commerce sites in 1999, up from 400,000 SMEs in 1998. The value of such SME transactions as a whole rose from $14 billion (1998) to $25 billion (1999), representing an increase of 79 percent.[11]

Some SMEs are aware that the novelty of online transactions might transform the way they conduct their overall workflows and operations. And they are willing to do some investment in e-commerce technology even though they still don't understand it very well. When something as important as the Internet revolution and e-commerce happen in the economy, the least any company can do is to be aware of it. Ignorance may result in missed opportunities and unforeseen competitive threats.

Why Electronic Commerce?

For customers, the advantages of online transactions through the Internet are striking. Buyers can easily compare the prices and conditions of different suppliers of products or services. And they can locate suppliers anywhere—in many cases in another country. There is no sales pressure,[12] and the search can be leisurely conducted at the customer's own pace. The amount of detailed information available about suppliers and goods is much greater online and can be accessed at the user's discretion. There are no business hours, which means that people can shop online at any hour or day of the week and can ignore time-zone differences. Users also cherish anonymity: sex sites' products and services, for instance, constitute approximately 10 percent of all retail business online, according to Forrester Research. And there are no transport problems such as traffic jams and bad weather—at least from the consumer's perspective. All of these reasons account for the explosion in the number of Internet users.

Some of these factors are also true for other kinds of nonstorefront commerce, such as telephone orders from catalogs and TV ads. But there are at least these crucial differences: the Web is interactive, it has full images, *and* the user is in control. Telephone ordering is interactive too, of course, but to a very limited degree, and telephones cannot show images. And with the replacement of live customer-service representatives with recorded voice menu systems ("press 49 for imported cheeses . . ."), telephone ordering has become much less pleasant and sometimes even annoying.[13]

Therefore, the beauty of the Internet's capacity for interaction is that the user controls every aspect of the transaction. If and when the user decides to leave a site, he or she can leave or branch out instantly: it's the user's choice. Advertisements are not forced on the user, who can always decide to exit and do something else or look for another site that is more interesting. The Internet is intrinsically different from the other forms of transactions in that it shifts the balance of power toward the consumer.

The typical online shopper has been identified (see also The User Profile, in chapter 2). In the United States, that shopper is male, is a college graduate in his forties, makes over $70,000 a year, and lives in the suburbs of a major metropolitan area, according to a survey of 1,000 online shoppers conducted by Binary Compass Enterprises.[14] Men constitute 60 to 70 percent of online buyers. Businesses can target this general audience or specific segments of it. Therefore, buyers will have at their disposal either general-interest sites or a kind of "village" where each buyer feels he or she belongs in.

Regulatory Framework

The U.S. government has come up with a "Global E-Commerce Framework."[15] The document states five principles that federal agencies need to follow when dealing with U.S. Internet issues. Considering the economic weight of the United States in international trade, the following directives will shape the way e-commerce is going to unfold worldwide:

· The private sector should lead;

· There should be no new taxes, tariffs, or unnecessary regulations;

· The government should restrict its role to establishing a simple legal environment for commerce;

· There should be no extension of the past regulatory framework for radio, TV, and telecommunications to the Internet;

· The Internet is a global marketplace, and the legal framework should be valid regardless of geographical jurisdiction.

A week after these directives were issued, ministers from twenty-nine European countries who were meeting in Bonn adopted the "Bonn Declaration on Global Information Networks."[16] Although more cautious than the U.S. declaration, the European declaration follows the basic premises of the U.S. framework. France is the most critical among the European countries, since many French officials see the Internet as a sophisticated form of the "American cultural invasion."[17] But the trend is in the direction of an international "free-trade zone" for e-commerce on the Internet.

The Four Steps in the Purchasing Process

Purchasing is a four-step process of search, order, payment, and delivery, and in an electronic transaction one or more of these steps are conducted online. In fact, the development and widespread use of the Internet are transforming all four of these steps into online operations, as shown in figure 3.1.

The figure shows that online searching has progressed further than ordering, payment, and delivery. Ordering online is becoming more popular, and more and more transactions are involving payment online. And eventually, at least for information-related products (the kinds of products defined by George Gilder as "bit products," such as music, as opposed to physical products or "atom products," such as bread),[18] delivery will also be completed online—as is already occurring with software and electronic documents, for example, that are sold on the Internet (see also Delivery, below).

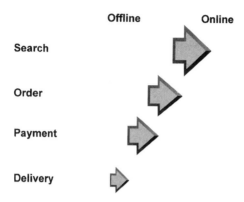

Figure 3.1
The Movement toward Online Transactions

As stated above, there is room for confusion in the definition of electronic commerce. To distinguish e-commerce from other electronic transactions, we define a transaction as constituting e-commerce when at least the ordering is done online. Consider the buyer who does all his prepurchase research about an item online and then goes to a store to buy or uses some other traditional shopping method. This kind of operation is not represented in any statistics of e-commerce and is not considered e-commerce here either. However, it is easy to recognize the crucial role of the internet exposure in the success of such sales.

Following this definition, searching for and ordering a pizza using the computer is e-commerce, even though payment and delivery are done offline, but ordering a product by telephone after searching for all the possibilities, specs, and prices on the Internet is not.

The following sections describe each of these four steps in more detail.

Search

Searches constitute one of the main activities conducted today on the Net, trailing only behind e-mail in terms of usage. Searching can be rewarding and yield interesting surprises—but it can be frustrating, too, given the overwhelming volume of available information.

A search can be conducted using several kinds of tools, most commonly housed in the browsers, search engines, content providers, and Internet service providers (ISPs).

Browsers

Browsers are software tools that access information on the Net by looking for the address, contacting the server where the information is stored (anywhere in the world), bringing the information into your computer, and "playing" it back to you (sometimes actually playing live audio or showing live video). The most popular browsers today are Netscape Navigator and Microsoft Explorer; each serves roughly half the market. Although technically speaking they are not search tools, when launched in your computer they take you to their own homepage (although the user can easily change this feature), which has search, content, and access facilities, blurring the distinction between them and the other tools presented below.

Search Engines

Search engines are software tools that try to match the keywords about a subject provided by the user with the keywords and actual text on existing indexed Web pages on the Net. The best matches are then rated and displayed to the user with the appropriate links so that the user can access the information immediately.

In the struggle to get users' attention, search engines' main Web pages have become premium real estate for advertisers, since many of these pages have a very high rate of exposure to the users (a common rating term is *eyeball*, or the number of people who see a page). The main search engines today are Yahoo!, Lycos, Alta Vista, Excite, and Infoseek. One indication of how seriously large companies regard the Internet is that between 1999 and 2000 Lycos was bought by Terra Networks, part of the large Spanish telecommunications conglomerate Telefonica; AltaVista (as part of Digital) by Compaq and then by CMGI; Excite by @Home (which is part of AT&T); and Infoseek by Disney.

One area of concern with using search engines is the accuracy of the results. The companies that run search engines survive on advertising. Once the user selects a subject—for example, high-quality car stereo systems—the search engine might direct him not to the Web site of the company that best fits his demand for quality but to the one that bids highest for the first position in the search results generated by any queries about car stereo systems. Trust—a vital component in the development of e-commerce—might suffer a blow if this arrangement of placement in exchange for pay is not made clear to the user.

Goto.com is a company that sells ranking positions. The arguable rationale in defense of paid ranking is that the companies that are willing to pay more to be listed first are the ones that users are most likely to be interested in anyway. The method and aim of this particular business model are clear. The company pays partners that point to its site 2 cents per visit. Considering that some subjects can generate as much as $2 per page-view in revenues from charges on click-throughs, the company hopes to turn a good profit somewhere in the near future.[19]

There are also data-mining tools that search the search engines and display the overall results. The use of search engines for particular business purposes is explained in more detail in chapter 7.[20]

Content Providers

The best-known content provider is the U.S. company America Online (AOL). Although it began as a proprietary access service provider, it soon became part of the more community-spirited Internet scheme: anyone can go to the site, and only a few services are reserved exclusively for members. The second-largest company, Prodigy, which is a bit more oriented to the business community, is now part of the AOL group. The merge or takeover of the Time Warner group by AOL in 2000 added tremendous strength to its content. Microsoft also tried to set up a proprietary service but succumbed eventually to the Internet juggernaut. Its service MSN can also be accessed by anyone.[21]

Internet Service Providers (ISPs)

Internet service providers, known as ISPs, are companies that provide access to the Internet for a monthly subscription of between $20 and $40. There is a movement in several countries, such as the United Kingdom and Brazil, for free service. ISPs in general started with the idea of providing an Internet "dial tone" to the user, without any information associated with it. For the same reasons described above, the high traffic on their homepages transformed ISPs into valuable vehicles for advertising, and they began to add content and become similar to the other tools.

New Developments

The differences between the Web sites of the main browsers, search engines, content providers, and ISPs are becoming superficial. It is probably more accurate today to refer to them all as information providers or *portals* to the Internet. Each can be used for searching, either directly or indirectly, for product information, current news, stock quotes, weather, and so on.

Ordering

It is now possible to order many different kinds of products and services directly from vendors. The best-selling goods online today, as was shown above, are travel, computer products, end-user products such as books and magazines, and music and entertainment products. From the customer's perspective, the e-commerce experience depends on the chosen method used to conduct the purchase, as explained below.

Online Companies

The most notable examples of e-commerce today are the online bookstores such as Amazon.com. This company is usually referred to as the poster child for e-commerce.[22] The company started selling books over the Internet and in a little over three years managed to produce annualized revenues of $1 billion. During the Christmas season of 1998 alone, Amazon added 1 million new customers and shipped 8 million items.[23] And many of these orders came from repeat customers, indicating high customer satisfaction. In the beginning of 2000, Amazon was adding 1 million new customers per month and had 20 million customers generating $2 billion in annualized sales. The rapid and amazing growth of the company led to its stunning valuation on the New York Stock Exchange, where the company's market value topped that of all U.S. bookstores combined even after the 2000 correction.

Amazon's phenomenal success made traditional booksellers uneasy. Barnes & Noble filed a libel suit in 1997 against Amazon, demanding that they dropped the slogan "earth's biggest bookstore." Apart from the marketing and legal wrangle, one interesting aspect of the dispute was the discussion about what constitutes a bookstore. If Amazon did not keep a single book in a warehouse, could it still be called a bookstore? (In fact, to promote speedy delivery Amazon does keep a warehouse stocked with the most sought-after titles.) As e-commerce moves forward, more and more of these questions and conflicts will emerge. Businesses and individuals are discovering that the Internet is a medium that changes the way we communicate in a profound and definitive way. After the initial success of Amazon, traditional booksellers followed suit. Barnes & Noble opened its electronic bookstore in 1997, and Borders did so in 1998. Amazon, at the same time, expanded its activities to other areas like CDs, toys, and medicines.[24]

The PC makers, especially those in the mail-order business, were among the first to explore the new medium. Dell Computer, for instance, is selling more than $20 million a day online—more than 30 percent of its total sales.[25] The same is true of Gateway 2000, a competing manufacturer in the mail-order business. The larger brand names are moving quickly to catch up, and today you can buy a desktop or notebook computer online directly from IBM, HP, Compaq, Toshiba, or other companies.

But the electronic marketplace has expanded well beyond books and PCs. Today so many companies all over the world are offering their products and services online that online customers can find fish from Chile, orchids from Singapore, wine from France, and gems or coffee from Brazil: the list grows daily.[26]

One business most likely to be an early winner is online ticketing, which is already the best-selling item in the United States.[27] Since the ticket business had been conducted largely by phone before, it is an ideal candidate to switch from voice to the Net. According to Bear Sterns, the revolution is already in full motion: in the first half of 1999, 1,800 offline travel agents went out of business. The number of jobs in the sector is expected to be cut eventually by at least 25 percent.[28] Online travel sales, on the other hand, are predicted to grow to $30 billion by 2003.

Ticketmaster, the previous leader in telephone booking, is still the leader in online sales of tickets for concerts and events. But after a few years of experimenting with ticket sales through the Internet, Ticketmaster decided to expand its reach into travel ticketing, which is a much larger market with powerful players. Who will succeed in this new market of travel reservation on the Net? Traditional travel agencies? Online ticketing from businesses such as Ticketmaster? Startups from the Internet age, such as Trip.com?[29] Risk and opportunity go hand in hand when a significant technological change takes place, and this important sector bears watching.

Electronic Catalogs

The catalog business is well developed in the United States and in many other countries. People receive printed listings of a wide range of product offerings at home and at work. Catalogs come in various formats: magazine, book, newspaper, loose sheets, leaflets—anything that will attract attention. In the United States alone, 132 million people (69 percent of the American adult population) use this form of commerce, and they are potential buyers in the electronic age. Women account for the majority of buyers at 73 million. These numbers refer to all buyers of products sold through television ads, catalogs, mail order, and, more and more, the Internet.

Some of these traditional catalog companies jumped onto the Web in an effort to retain their cherished customers. The largest one, according to the NPD Group, is QVC. QVC's online shopping service claims to have been profitable since its beginning (1997), taking about 1 percent of all the Web's traffic and selling over $1 million a month over the Net. Another large one, Home Shopping Network, tried to increase its stake on the Internet in 1999 through the purchase of search-engine company Lycos by its parent company USA Networks, but the deal did not go through.[30]

Virtual Malls and Superstores

One of the main forms of electronic commercial exposure is the "virtual mall." A shopping mall in the United States (also called a shopping center in many countries) is a large shopping precinct with tens, sometimes hundreds, of shops of all kinds, normally with easy access by car and ample parking. In addition to the shops, malls also have common areas (such as food courts) and services and ammenities (such as cinemas). The electronic equivalent is called the *virtual mall*. A virtual mall is a common electronic address also for tens, sometimes hundreds of virtual shops, of all kinds, where the customer can "walk" around, "enter" the shops, and select products or services. Some of these malls even have graphic effects that give the user the impression of actually "seeing" the shop windows and displays. Common areas can provide electronic services or even physical ones—such as ordering pizzas, for instance.

New virtual malls are sprouting everywhere. There are dozens of examples in the United States and abroad—Cybershop, for computer-related items; Netmarket or Shop4, for anything under the sun; or Shopping, if you like bargain hunting.[31]

IBM was one notable exception when it decided to shut down its online shopping mall, World Avenue, in July 1997. IBM explained the surprising decision as arising from a need to concentrate more on the company's core businesses. The mall was doing fine but was contributing little to help sell more of IBM's products. Later that year, though, IBM came back online, launching a series of products for e-commerce in an eight-page advertisement in several U.S. newspapers.[32] The company's president stated that the whole company's strategy would be based on e-business as from 1998. In that year, half of the advertising budget went into banners online, and IBM had a large increase in the company's name "recall" (remembrance of the brand name by customers). Today, IBM's small red "e" in the term "e-business" that is used in all of the company's marketing campaigns is almost as recognizable by consumers as the traditional blue logo of the company.

The virtual mall is not an unqualified success, however. In all its forms it is still trying to mimic the real (physical) mall—an environment familiar to customers but rather limited in its scope. As so often happens with new technologies, we might be applying a new medium (the Internet) to an old paradigm (the shopping mall). The eventual outcome of the ongoing developments in electronic commerce might be very different from today's mall. But since no radically different model has yet materialized, we have continued to use the same old ideas. The bottom line is that e-commerce is clearly a winner but that the virtual mall is only one of several possible alternatives for implementing it.

Another variation on the virtual mall is the *electronic superstore.* As in a major department store, shoppers can buy nearly anything, from pencils to boats, but the electronic superstore can be even more diversified since it has no need for consumer-appealing real estate. Some of these stores charge a monthly or annual membership fee for special features; others do not. One of the membership-based services is Net Market.[33] Besides selling its products at a low price, the company offers additional services such as an auction site, a flea market, and an intelligent search mechanism that helps users narrow their focus on products based on price range, manufacturer, or other characteristic and then compare features of those products side by side on the screen.

"Shopping the Shops"
The well-known consulting firm Arthur Andersen opened a shopping-the-shops service that mimics the "shopping-around" method of finding the best price. Pieces of software known as *software agents,* or cookies (but see also Privacy in chapter 4) collect data from the user's buying pattern and can help the user search for products that are of particular interest.[34] One special feature is the bargain finder: it looks through the existing electronic malls for the best price on a specific product such as a CD or a book. For a small company, the mall venue can be a substitute for a brand name, since buyers can be drawn into the shop through this process based on their interest in a particular product, not a brand name.

Some superstores such as Net Market also offer this service for some kinds of products. Users subscribe to the service, and the company promises that it will always beat the price of the competition. The superstore may offer a book, for instance, at a given price and then compare its price to that of the competition (other online bookstores). If its own price is higher, it is instantly lowered. This service is also available for other kinds of goods and services, from cars to travel.

In these trying times of e-commerce, several companies are offering free services to users and trying to make ends meet with paid advertisements only. Such is the case with Compare.net.[35] The company helps the user find not only the best prices but also the specifications that meet the user's needs. After comparing specifications from different vendors, the user can then proceed to buy online from the chosen vendor.

International Efforts

The e-commerce phenomenon is spreading globally. In the United Kingdom, even the conservative Barclays Bank has opened its own Barclay Square, with fifteen virtual shops. Ten percent of its reported 300,000 customers come from outside the United Kingdom, and goods can be delivered worldwide.

Electronic commerce is also becoming important in continental Europe. France's situation, however, is unique: having first arrived at a limited kind of e-commerce with their proprietary system, Minitel, the French are lagging behind in the adoption of the Internet and other new technologies. The situation is now changing, but France is only fifteenth in the world in Internet penetration, despite having the fifth-largest telecommunications operator (France Telecom). Germany is moving much faster—65 percent of German businesses have access to the Net—and is gaining ground as the European center for e-commerce.[36] Department stores and new specialized malls are already doing substantial businesses on the Net. Other examples can be found in other parts of the world.[37]

Payment

We defined e-commerce as an electronic transaction in which at least the ordering step is performed using a computer, regardless of how the first step—search—has been conducted. The two subsequent steps, payment and delivery, differentiate electronic transactions today, depending on how they are completed (see table 3.5).

Table 3.5
Different Forms of E-Commerce

Delivery	Payment Offline	Online
Offline	Services: hotel and ticket reservations Food: pizzas, sandwiches Other goods: flowers	Books, magazines, CDs, DVDs, papers, office supplies
Online	Free try-out: payments and invoices later	Today: software, music Tomorrow: ?

The simplest form of e-commerce happens when the product or service is ordered on the Net but payment or delivery—such as making a hotel reservation or ordering pizza—is not completed online. Although some of these transactions require that the buyer provide a credit-card number as a payment guarantee to the merchant, the actual commitment of the buyer is completed only, for example, at the hotel check-in desk or on delivery of the food. In this case, both payment for and delivery of the services are done offline.

Less common is online delivery (say, in a try-out-first scheme) followed by a bill that is delivered later by regular mail. The products and services that use this scheme today are usually software tools or information from a content provider. In the future, something like a work of art could be viewed, listened to, or read and then paid for offline (see Delivery, below).

But the most popular Net transaction today is online ordering and payment, and offline delivery—of books, CDs, groceries, office supplies, and so on. This type of transaction represents the direct transposition of the mail-order business to the Internet: a physical product is delivered to your home or office. Depending on the rate at which e-commerce grows, however, the number of transactions could be enormous, altering the overall picture of retailing today (see What's Next?, below). Package-delivery companies such as FedEx, UPS, and DHL would be direct beneficiaries of such a massive increase in online ordering and offline delivery.

In the fourth kind of transaction, payment and delivery are done online. This amazing development, unparalleled before, is discussed in Delivery, below.

Goods and services ordered online can be paid for using traditional credit cards, electronic payments, or e-cash.[38] The state of the art and the new developments in these three payment methods are discussed below.

Credit Cards

For cross-border transactions, the most common method of payment will likely continue to be the credit card, considering that the two major companies, VISA and MasterCard, already have between them over 1 billion accounts. Both are very active in new developments for e-commerce. But security is still a major concern. Although the use of credit-cards is commonplace today, with no guarantees of security (the waiter or shop attendant often disappears to the back of the premises with your card for several minutes, for example), many users still experience some level of discomfort about giving their credit-card numbers over the Net. It is possible to argue that the least secure place may be the vendors' servers where the credit-card numbers of clients are kept—because break-ins there are much more profitable. Nonetheless, on the Internet, users are ultimately in control; they are demanding additional levels of security, and many companies are providing them.

CyberCash launched its credit-card purchases service in 1995. Both the buyer and the merchant must be registered with CyberCash to participate. The buyer sends a message to the merchant to place the order, and the merchant sends back an electronic invoice. The user appends credit-card information to the invoice and sends it to the merchant using CyberCash's software, which encrypts the information. The merchant sends the invoice to CyberCash, which in turn clears the transaction with the credit-card company, as in any typical offline purchase. After the approval, CyberCash sends the confirmation to the merchant, which can then deliver the goods. The difference between this service and a typical credit-card transaction is the added level of security provided by the CyberCash software.[39] The merchant is never given the buyer's credit-card number. The transaction procedure is explained

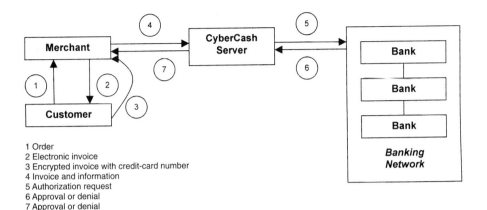

1 Order
2 Electronic invoice
3 Encrypted invoice with credit-card number
4 Invoice and information
5 Authorization request
6 Approval or denial
7 Approval or denial

Figure 3.2
An Online Payment Using Cybercash Software
Source: Setsuko Minami Kawa, "Changing Money: Cash and Cards, Virtual and Electronic." © 1998 by the President and Fellows of Harvard College.
Note: The merchant never knows the customer's credit-card number.

in figure 3.2. (Also see the discussion of CyberCoin under Electronic Payments, below.)

A simpler but also effective system is to file a credit-card number with a company that acts as an intermediary between the merchant and the buyer. When the buyer makes a purchase, the merchant sends a message to the intermediary requesting payment. The intermediary sends an e-mail to the buyer for confirmation of the deal. Once it gets the confirmation, the intermediary completes the credit-card transaction.[40] In this system, no credit-card numbers are floating around on the Net, and the security of the transaction theoretically is increased. But whether or not these transactions are actually more secure, the user has a perception of greater security.

First Virtual Holdings (FVH) started this kind of service. Users register their credit-card numbers with FVH in a secure mode and only once. Then they get an ID number for electronic transactions. During a purchase, this number is sent to the merchant, which confirms the number with FVH. FVH, in turn, confirms the transaction by e-mail with the user. If the user approves it, FVH proceeds with the credit-card clearance, again in the traditional way, and returns the approval to the merchant. Once payment is approved, the merchant proceeds to deliver the goods.

Some of the largest financial and other companies involved in e-commerce have agreed on a protocol for secure transactions called *secure electronic transaction* (SET). The SET protocol is a collection of encryption and security specifications used as an industrywide standard for ensuring secure payment transactions over the Internet.[41]

It is not clear which payment system will become most popular with users. But credit cards, used either directly or through some kind of intermediary that allows for security, will be the standard payment method for e-commerce for some time to come.

Electronic Payments

As with most issues related to the Internet, consensus has not been reached on e-commerce terminology. For our purposes, however, we can define electronic payment as any kind of payment (except for credit cards) done over the Net in which money moves from the buyer's bank account to the merchant's, either directly or through an intermediary that has the authority to clear transactions. And we can define e-cash as the currency involved in any financial transaction that moves money electronically from the user's bank account to his own computer or e-wallet from which the user can make payments directly to a merchant or any other party.

In 1993, a consortium of financial companies in the United States launched the "electronic check" project as part of the Financial Services Technology Consortium (FSTC), aimed at providing the means to send a check securely over the Internet. The buyer receives a removable PC card—the small boards, the size of a bank card, that the user can insert into a laptop—from the issuing bank with information about his account. This card is his "checkbook." Through the computer that has the PC card the buyer can send a merchant an electronic check that is then sent to the merchant's bank for clearance. Once the transaction is completed, records on the electronic check store information about the transaction, dates, and delivery, so that all parties (user, merchant, and bank) can update their databases with the new transaction automatically.

In 1995, a full-service online bank called Security First Network Bank (SFNB) was created. Customers can keep checking and savings accounts, move money between them, pay bills, transfer money electronically or through a real check by mail—in short, everything that they can do through traditional banks. In fact, most traditional banks offer home-banking solutions today, and there is in effect no difference between SFNB and the home-banking tool of a traditional bank. Being a virtual bank, however, SFNB can afford to offer competitive prices for services because it does not pay for the overhead of tellers and customer-service employees as traditional banks do. The success of SFNB attracted the attention of traditional banks, and in 1997 it was bought by the Royal Bank of Canada.[42]

Another service supported by the CyberCash company is CyberCoin. Both the user and the merchant must be registered with the service to use it. The service was set up for small-change purchases over the Net, such as purchase of information content. These transactions typically are between 25 cents and $10, making the cost of a full credit-card trans-action prohibitive. The user sets up the service by downloading money from a bank or credit-card account into a virtual CyberCash "wallet," where the money is converted into CyberCoins. When the user pays the merchant with CyberCoins, the merchant deposits them into a "wallet," from which the money can be uploaded to its normal bank account. CyberCash claims that the service is effective, secure, and cheap. It costs from 8 to 25 cents for transactions involving from 25 cents to $10. This service could also be classified as e-cash (see below)—but according to our definition above, the money is not transferred to the user, and so no e-cash is actually being generated.[43]

Other systems and sets of tools for electronic commerce and cash payments are under development.[44]

E-Cash

E-cash is evolving in various forms. In one of them the user buys e-cash from his or her own bank account or credit card. This "virtual money" is stored in the user's computer and can be used for purchases over the Net, but only from virtual shops that subscribe to the same system. The user and the merchant must both be registered with the service, and each participant receives an ID number and password. An interesting feature of this form of payment is that the user remains anonymous to the merchant. But the merchant company is identified when it deposits the e-cash from the transaction into the bank that issued the e-cash.[45]

Another option is the so-called smart card. One of the main developments of this type of card to date is MasterCard's Mondex.[46] The system is undergoing trials in pilot projects all over the world. The main component of the system is a plastic card that looks like an ordinary credit card but contains a microchip; in this way the card becomes a mini-computer that can exchange information with other computers. The user downloads money from a personal account and stores it on the card, which can then be used for purchases, limited to the stored amount, from the merchants that accept that particular card. Another feature of this system is that the user can also get a small electronic "wallet" that can read and show the remaining balance on the card and even check the last ten transactions. The wallet also allows the user to transfer currency from one card to another (for instance, from mother's card to daughter's).

Other systems have also been developed. The largest credit-card company, VISA, developed VISA Cash,[47] which is currently undergoing trials in several cities around the world. The system was first tested at the 1996 Olympic Games in Atlanta. Like its competitor Mondex, the system allows the user to load cash into its microchip and to use it to make purchases from merchants that have the proper card reader. One of the largest trials was conducted in New York's Upper West Side, with several ATM locations where the card could be loaded and hundreds of merchants that could accept it. Unlike Mondex, however, VISA cash does not allow for individual transfers of money between two users. The New York trial met with limited success, mainly because it was not accepted outside the trial region. VISA is now conducting a more extensive trial in the town of Celebration, Florida, where broader geographic coverage is expected to produce more positive results.

The simplest version of the e-cash card is the dumb disposable card, which is growing in popularity. Like the basic telephone card, it has no microchip but can store financial information magnetically. Thus, the user can load, for instance, $100 from an ATM machine to the card and spend the money wherever the card is accepted. Once the money is spent, the card is thrown away. Although less versatile than the smart card, the disposable card is more secure, from the user's perspective: if you lose the card, the actual financial loss is limited to the currency remaining in the card. And it is completely anonymous, of course.

With so many cards already in use today, the introduction of e-cash might seem simply to add to the confusion. However, some of these new technologies will likely be combined into multipurpose cards. Look, for instance, for debit/credit/cash smart cards, disposable gift cards from merchants (similar to today's coupons), identity/personal information/ credit smart cards, and others. Identity cards (although fiercely opposed in the United States) may become popular around the world and can be used to allow access to buildings or even for electronic voting and personal identification in general.

Security and privacy are obvious concerns in relation to payment. These topics are discussed in chapter 4.

Delivery

Of the types of transactions discussed above, the newest (albeit not yet commonly used) and most striking operation involves the payment and delivery of goods online (see table 3.5). Apart from a few transactions concerning software, this newest form of commerce is not yet widely employed, since it has only recently been made possible by the Net. Other goods that lend themselves to online delivery include artistic or craft-related products, such as music, painting, or recipes. Want to listen to the latest tune from your favorite singer? Turn to her home page, transfer the contents to your computer, and play it back locally. Nothing "physical" is produced—there are no packages, no delivery in the traditional sense, no taxes—and yet you receive and use the product. Payment to the merchant (perhaps the artist, musician, or author) will be made through some kind of e-cash (as discussed above), and the deal will involve only two people. No record (in both senses of the word) of the transaction needs to exist.

There are important differences between online and offline deliveries. In offline delivery, represented by the bookstore and the theater ticket examples (in Ordering, above), the Net is used for marketing and visual (or sound) display by the merchant and for virtual comparison, selection, and ordering by the consumer. The European Commission calls this *indirect electronic commerce.*[48] The goods are delivered in the traditional way, very similar to today's huge mail-order market.[49] In the other, a completely new form of commerce is created, eliminating the intermediaries. This is *direct electronic commerce.* If statistics for the first group are difficult to project, what about the second group, for which there is hardly any history?

Electronic transactions involving small amounts of money—small-change transactions (micropayments)—are rare today but could become one of the most important developments on the Net. The opportunities in this area are virtually limitless. The number of transactions can be enormous, and a new song, a timely picture, or a short video could generate millions of dollars in revenues.

Business-to-Business Transactions

In any supply chain, information is vital. And in doing business across boundaries, the Internet could be the perfect tool to track inventory. A study by Arthur Andersen points out that 30 percent of potential customers leave the store because the product they want to buy is not available then and there, which dramatically demonstrates the importance of the exchange of current information between suppliers and retail stores.[50] Supervox, the French supplier of do-it-yourself goods, routinely checks stock updates to ensure that its shelves will remain well stocked.[51] The orchid producer in Singapore that is described in chapter 5 is now organizing an "extranet" with its suppliers to be able to offer discounts and updated reports about their flowers to their end consumers all over the world.[52]

Business-to-business transactions on the Internet will become even more important than business-to-consumer transactions in terms of revenues, as we have seen already. Its main advantages are the reduction of purchasing costs, better control of inventory, more efficiency in client services, reduction of marketing and sales costs, and the opening of new business opportunities. And the exchange of information will be no less vital in these transactions. Purchasing supplies and components company-to-company over the Net is expected to become increasingly commonplace in the near future.

General Electric, one of the largest U.S. corporations, expects to conduct a substantial portion of its business from now on, online on its corporate trading network. The network is designed to improve and tighten relationships among its component companies, clients, and suppliers. This trend is evident throughout the industry. The movement to go online has been driven not only by marketing and sales goals but—and perhaps most important—by the desire for improved relations, service, and responsiveness to partners involved in the companies' business procedures.

What's Next?

For those still skeptical about the potential and the real impact of electronic commerce, I offer a practical example. In the early 1960s, people gathered around the entrance of a Barclays Bank branch in London to watch the workings of a new marvel: the electronic cash dispenser. Today automatic teller machines (ATMs) can be found almost everywhere (even some developing countries such as Brazil, once plagued by inflation, were early adopters of the technology) and can perform most bank transactions instantly. Not only do ATMs offer great convenience to users, but the cost of an ATM operation to the bank is 80 percent less than that conducted in a physical storefront by a teller. Looking back to the 1960s, how many people would have believed then that thirty years later—we would take automated banking for granted?

Society adopts successful new technologies in stages. First comes amazement and perhaps skepticism, then come the early adopters, the followers, and finally the mass market. Eventually, everyone feels as if the novelty has been around forever. Although many of us remember a time without photocopiers, most people feel today as if the ubiquitous machines have been with us forever. The PC, introduced in 1981, is another example. The Internet, a technology that has been in commercial use for only a few years, is now reaching the mass market. The same is likely to happen to e-commerce. Although e-commerce is still in the early adopters' phase, ten years from now we might feel that it has been around forever.

The actual revenues from e-commerce are still small compared with direct mail or catalog sales. But the number of users with full access to the Internet is also small. How will e-commerce change in the next five to ten years, when over 1 billion people will be on the Net using 5 to 6 billion access devices and when users will be much more computer literate than the current generation of users?

Major obstacles on the road to full electronic commerce remain, though—including the need for secure transactions and the buildup of trust between companies and between companies and customers (see chapter 4). But e-commerce is already gaining a strong foothold in many areas.

Skeptics see the development of e-commerce as overhyped—the fact that AOL is worth more than General Motors or that Yahoo! is worth more than Boeing is offered as evidence—but the prodigious growth rate of the sector is unquestionable. The question today is not if but when is e-commerce taking off? Rich Karlgaard, editor of *Forbes ASAP* magazine, sums up the situation in an insightful article in the magazine's April 1998 edition.[53] He uses the metaphor of the hockey stick and asks if we are coming to the inflection point in the revenue curve where growth is no longer linear but zooms up. The retail sector in the United States involves $2.5 trillion. What percentage of this economic activity will move online? Even a mere 5 percent would amount to $125 billion. Globally, let us assume it is double that number: $250 billion. Who will be the beneficiaries of these impressive revenues—traditional retailers, catalogs, newcomers? How many times will we witness the Davids, such as newcomer Amazon.com, challenging the Goliaths, such as Barnes & Noble and Borders, which then need between two and three years to counterattack? And what will be the outcome of these commercial wars once the buyers make up their minds?

E-commerce raises many questions, most of them still unanswered. But e-commerce is one of the most exciting new economic developments to watch in this new century. Those bold and fortunate enough will not only watch but play that game too.

Recommended Further Reading

Leebaert, D., ed. *The Future of the Electronic Marketplace.* Cambridge, MA: MIT Press, 1999.

Evans, P., and Wurster, T. *Blown to Bits.* Boston: Harvard Business School Press, 2000.

Westland, J., and Clark, T. *Global Electronic Commerce.* Cambridge, MA: MIT Press, 1999.

4

Are We Ready? Main Obstacles to International Trade for Small Companies

We are surrounded by insurmountable opportunities.
—William Thorsell

Introduction

New opportunities are emerging for small and medium-size enterprises (SMEs) in the international market. Although it has never been easy for a small company to export goods or services, now it is possible. And that is a significant change. There remain many obstacles, though, including cultural differences, limits imposed by local and international law, and, in many countries, inadequate infrastructure for transport and communications.

As a framework for discussion, consider what occurs in cross-border e-commerce transactions. The term *cross-border* takes on a new meaning in the context of e-commerce. When products or services are delivered online, where exactly are the national borders? Think back to chapter 3's example of the Chinese painting stored on a Singapore server, sold electronically to a Mexican customer, who has a U.S. Internet account, pays by a Spanish credit card and prints a copy of the painting on his home printer. Which country's GDP gets credit for this transaction? Who records the transaction, and how? Who (if anyone) pays taxes, where, and in what currency? What actions can be taken if commercial disputes arise?

This chapter discusses all of these issues and indicates, wherever discernible, how each obstacle to international e-commerce might be removed in the near future.

Table 4.1
Worldwide Distribution of PCs

Region	PCs per 1,000 People
Developed countries	264
Eastern Europe and Central Asia	50
Latin America and the Caribbean	33
Middle East and North Africa	10
East Asia and Pacific	7
South Asia	2
Sub-Saharan Africa	2

Source: World Bank (1999).[1]

Infrastructure and Logistics

Computer Density

Contrary to what many of us are led to believe, computers are not available everywhere. The distribution of PCs—even more so than that of many other common appliances—is uneven at best. This holds true not only in developing countries but also in the richest (see table 4.1).[1]

The differences between regions are enormous. But even in developed countries, populations in economically deprived areas have limited access to computers. SMEs seeking international markets need to evaluate the real business opportunities in the specific part of the world they are interested in.

Internet Access

Just as computers are not evenly distributed worldwide, neither is telephone access (see table 4.2).[2] In fact, half the globe's people have never made a phone call and live more than 30 miles away from the nearest telephone.[3] What are the prospects for telecommunications—let alone e-commerce—in the countries in Sub-Saharan Africa with sixteen telephone lines per 1,000 people, when affluent countries have 500 telephone lines per 1,000 people?

Telephone lines and PCs constitute the most basic infrastructure for any activity related to the Internet. Some countries are so far behind that they may leapfrog fixed-wire service altogether into cellular service. Building that infrastructure may be more cost-effective as the wireless

Table 4.2
Worldwide Distribution of Telephone Lines

Region	Telephone Lines per 1,000 People
Developed countries	506
Eastern Europe and Central Asia	204
Latin America and the Caribbean	110
Middle East and North Africa	75
East Asia and Pacific	50
South Asia	18
Sub-Saharan Africa	16

Source: World Bank (1999).

Table 4.3
Distribution of Internet Users by Region (percent)

Region	2000	2005
North America	43.3%	30.3%
Western Europe	25.1	27.2
Asia and Pacific	20.6	24.8
Eastern Europe	3.1	6.6
Latin America	5.6	7.3
Middle East and Africa	2.3	3.8
	100%	100%

Source: *Computer Industry Almanac* (1999), in <http://www.c-1-2.com/199904iv.htm>.

world takes over and the prices for basic equipment become even less costly in the future.

Internet access today, however, is mostly done through the fixed-wire network and, although still sparse, is growing rapidly. See table 4.3 for the worldwide distribution of Internet access.

Until 1999, when the rest of the world started to catch up, more than half the users of the Internet were in the United States. As shown in table 4.3, the world's Internet population is going to increase everywhere, in both absolute and relative terms, and the United States, which led the initial wave of users, will claim a smaller percentage of the world's Internet users.

Table 4.4
Per Capita Internet Penetration

Rating by per-Capita Penetration	Countries or Regions	Percent of Population with Internet Access
1	Norway, Finland, Sweden	30–35%
2	United States, Canada, Australia	20–29
3	United Kingdom, Germany, Netherlands	9–19
4	Japan, Taiwan	8
5	Developing and transition countries	<8

Source: UNCTAD (1999).[3]

On a per-capita basis, most surprisingly, the best-connected regions are the Nordic countries, not the United States, followed by the other Organization for Economic Cooperation and Development (OECD) countries (including the United States), the leading Asian nations, and the majority of the developing countries (see table 4.4).

Access is one thing, though, and business is another. Until the end of 1998, 93 percent of all the real business (commercial transactions) conducted on the Web was related to U.S.-based sites. But as more people gain access to the Internet and use it for day-to-day applications, e-business will increasingly be based and conducted in other parts of the world as well.

An SME business strategy must first determine whether the target audience is currently accessible through fixed-wire communications and, if it is not, prepare for the next likely step in the technological evolution of that region. As broadband technologies emerge, the strategy needs to determine what kind of access the target audience has. To establish and maintain contact with customers, you must always be aware of their current—and anticipated—technological capabilities and, in many countries, the possibility of a technological leapfrog.

Serving the User

Once users find your site, you have only a fleeting opportunity to grab their attention. You may instinctively lean toward using eye-catching graphics and text-heavy, complex designs, but there are advantages and risks to this approach. Complicated graphic elements that take forever to download may cause your customers to lose interest, and excessive text with too few graphic elements may have the same effect. One rule of thumb is to use graphics sparingly. Test your site from a dial-up line using the current modem speed; if it works well under those circumstances, your customers should be satisfied with the response. If the dial-up is not successful, it's back to the drawing board. Fancy embellishments might work well on the local network at your office but result in a disappointing and frustrating experience for the user.

You have to be prepared for success, too. A sudden burst of access to your company's server might provoke breakdowns and outages. The operators of the *Britannica* site, for instance, decided one day to offer free access, and the avalanche of users caused the service to collapse. It took *Britannica* several days to fix the problem. The same problem occurred at the auction site eBay, the *National Geographic* site, and several other sites that could not cope with an unprecedented level of activity.[4] Recent research by Jupiter Communications showed that only 10 percent of existing sites would be prepared to double their level of activity in a day. The good (and bad) news is that on the Internet, doubling activity in a short period is quite possible. Be prepared in advance for this level of success to take advantage of sudden opportunities.

Transport and Distribution of Goods and Services

Goods and services offered on the Web can be, in the words of Internet guru George Gilder, either "bit products" or "atom products." Bit products are created and stored in a digital format, such as software, music, electronic literature, images, and other downloadable goods. They can be transported directly over the Net, given the necessary bandwidth. But most products currently offered on the Internet are atom products, which are material and tangible. Delivery of these goods to the end user depends on a logistics network that is not, for the most part, in place on a worldwide scale. Existing transport structures were developed to accommodate business-to-business (B2B) needs and in general are expensive. They are viable only for the large quantities of goods that characterize B2B e-commerce.

But for business-to-consumer e-commerce, which generally involves small quantities and low-price items, transport infrastructure must still be created in many areas. Imagine, for example, a T-shirt produced in Malaysia and painted in Hong Kong for delivery to a customer in the outskirts of Paris. The producer in Malaysia ships a large volume of T-shirts to Hong Kong to be painted. But from that point on, transporting the T-shirt becomes an individual operation. The finished product has to be packaged and taken to a postal service, which will send it to a distribution center, where it will be bundled with other items for France. On arrival in France, the load will be separated, and the individual package with the T-shirt will go through the appropriate distribution channels until it is directed to its final destination.

Let us consider the magnitude of the problem:

• With the proliferation of e-commerce, geographical barriers to purchasing will dissolve, but the barriers to delivery may therefore be much more daunting than any company is currently prepared to handle. Some destinations may even be inaccessible by traditional means.

• The multistage process, which involves bundling for transportation, might increase delivery time to the point that the user might lose interest in the purchase—particularly if the credit-card transaction is cleared immediately and the delivery takes several weeks.

• Manipulation of the product in the various transport stages might mean repackaging to conform to local processes, increasing the risk of product damage.

• Costs can become prohibitive.

Challenging, isn't it? But think of this challenge as the start of a revolution in the distribution of goods and services. New delivery services and opportunities to devise innovative means of transport are available in the market, perhaps using some of the distribution networks already in place to deliver other things. Vint Cerf, one of the fathers of the Internet, commented, "During the gold rush, the first guy to become rich wasn't the one who found gold; it was the one who manufactured picks and shovels." No one is sure about which e-commerce companies will be the winners in the long run. But an effective and inexpensive transport service that delivers small packages around the world is a clear winner, regardless of the other players in the e-commerce race. Delivery of packages is one of the pick-and-shovel tools of this business and can be an excellent opportunity for startups. The newcomers would face competition, in many cases and in many countries, only from gigantic, cumbersome, slow, state-run postal monopolies.

Credit Cards and Foreign Currency

Credit cards are the most important and expedient means of payment for e-purchases today. Their use is widespread but—as with other forms of technology—is concentrated primarily in developed parts of the world.

In many countries, the use of foreign currency involves strict government controls that may hinder the development of cross-border business. For many international companies selling goods abroad, the best way to complete financial transactions is to keep an account at a foreign bank in the target country (where the buyer is located) that can handle the credit-card transactions and tie these operations to the legal system in the original country of the seller company. The money can then be used to buy things in that country or be internalized according to local rules.

VISA and MasterCard have already issued more than 1 billion cards, as we have already seen. But use of plastic money is geographically concentrated: half of all the credit cards issued are in the United States. Additionally, many Americans carry several cards in their wallet, whereas in many countries credit cards are used rarely, if at all. Even in developed countries such as Japan, consumers have but do not use credit cards: it is seen as an easy—and shameful—form of debt. But the overall growth is impressive: credit-card transactions jumped from 10 percent of all payment transactions in 1994 to 15 percent in 1998.[5] But the uneven distribution of credit cards in the world can affect online operations, depending on the target audience abroad.

Security

To flourish as a venue for business (relations) and commerce (transactions), the Internet must be—and must be perceived as being—safe. Once consumers in the United States began to lose their fears about using their credit cards to buy on the Internet, e-commerce turned from a technological curiosity into a fast-growing phenomenon and a part of everyday life.

Commerce is basically a swap in which each of the two parties involved has something that the other one wants. The swap is agreed on when the values that each party attributes to its object and to the object of the other party are equal. The transaction is realized when the two objects change hands. When one of the objects does not correspond to the description given or perceived by one of the parties during the negotiation process, problems can ensue. This misunderstanding might be due to an unintentional error or to fraud. An error can generally be resolved by the reciprocal return of the two swapped items or by replacing the unwanted item with another.

Fraud, on the other hand, must be prevented. For e-commerce to grow, there must be a secure means to avoid fraud. When the processing of an e-commerce transaction reaches the payment stage, most vendors use a protocol called secure-sockets layer (SSL) that guarantees that the data will be understood only by the addressee of the message. In the two most common browsers, an icon identifies this phase (in Internet Explorer, it is the closed lock; in Netscape, the key), and the secure server of the vendor is identified by a different code address, beginning with "https://." The message is cryptographed, and only the receiver of the message has the key to decode it. The key changes with every transaction, so it is practically impossible for strangers to decode its content. This mechanism provides security for the buyer.

But what about the vendor? How does the vendor know that the buyers are who they say they are? Security systems for e-commerce have been developed to take care of four basic requirements:

• *Authentication* allows one party to certify another's identity.

• *Integrity* guarantees that the original message has not been altered during transmission.

• *Nonrepudiation* guarantees that the message was sent and received, precluding arguments such as "I didn't order it" or "I didn't receive it."

• *Privacy* prevents third parties from reading the transmitted message.

Sophisticated cryptographic methods normally use two keys and involve certification of digital entities and signatures. The choice of a security mechanism is crucial in the development of an e-commerce site—especially because a buyer might use its own certification scheme, mainly in business-to-business applications. Small-business owners are advised to consult a cryptography specialist on such matters, since online security systems are beyond most business owners' scope of expertise.

The secure electronic transaction (SET) standard guarantees the four basic aspects of security for online transactions. Additionally, the SET protocol uses the credit-card company as an intermediary that interacts with the buyer for the financial data, so that the vendor does not know the buyer's credit-card information.

The U.S. government has opposed the export of American products that use "strong encryption" (128 bits) due to concerns about national security: terrorists and criminals, for instance, would communicate more safely. But this opposition has harmed American exports, though, and several groups are lobbying to reverse it. Legislators in some U.S. states are trying to act quickly in this matter to improve the business climate. California, for instance, now accepts a digital signature as being as valid as a hard-copy signature on a check.[6]

Internet Support Services

It would be difficult, and in many cases impractical, for a business to have all the necessary Internet support services in-house to support an entry into e-commerce. Most companies, and especially smaller ones, must have access to outside vendors for such services, including Web-site design, database support, Web hosting, Web server, and payment and security services. In the more technologically developed countries, these services are readily available and can be contracted out easily. But in most parts of the world, these services are sparse, when they are available at all.

Some services can be directly contracted abroad over the Internet itself. So company A can sell to company B a good or service for which it used parts and services from company C, the latter an Internet business in a third country. So the use of third-party vendors is one possible route. But for the e-commerce sector to thrive, the Internet support-services industry must develop and expand all over the world. In some countries, this industry might offer unparalleled opportunities, particularly for early entrants. It is impossible to predict which companies will come out on top in the e-commerce rush, but they will all need reliable Web support services. The specialized IT magazines like *PC Magazine*, *Byte*, and *Internet Weekly* conduct periodic surveys and rate the existing support services available on the Web.

People

It has been said that the three most important needs in many developing countries are, in order of importance, education, education, and education. In these high-tech times, this need takes on even greater significance. Developing countries generally lack people with the necessary skills to apply new technologies. Governments can play a vital role in future economic growth by investing in special educational and training programs targeting these new technologies. Small company owners, for their part, can push local governments into action using their political clout: small companies, when organized, represent significant political power.

Even in the developed world, the growth of the technological sector has been so rapid that the number of skilled workers is insufficient to effect the necessary transformation across companies and industries. U.S. immigration laws have been changed several times to allow American companies to hire foreign workers with technical skills that fill the existing gaps in the workforce.

For some developing countries, this demand for skilled help can be both a burden and a blessing, as India has proved in the software industry. Indian companies provide programming services that developed countries need and do so at a lower cost than companies based in those countries. There are other interesting considerations, as well. Engineering and related fields are more highly regarded by society as a whole in developing nations than they are in the developed world. The infrastructure for public services, for instance—roads, electricity, sewage, and telecommunications networks—is already established in the developed countries but is still under construction in developing regions. Engineers are in demand, well regarded, and well paid compared with workers in other professions. This environment encourages a concentration of talent in these fields that can easily be tapped by emerging technologies. Although technical skills are scarce, they may be of very good quality and can be used either internally or for the export market.

Legal Matters

Jurisdiction

One of the main advantages of the Internet over other means of communication is that there are no barriers to entry; one can access a public universal resource locator (URL)—an Internet address—from anywhere on the globe. Such wide accessibility raises an important legal question: When a site is published on the Web and made available to the public, is the site owner subject to the laws of all the countries where it can be accessed? Is the owner liable in courts worldwide?

There is no clear answer to these questions. As with most issues related to the Internet, any major innovation demands new regulations. In an e-commerce transaction, especially across borders, many countries may be involved, and the situation can become complex. In the painting example that was cited above, what action could be taken if something went wrong in this multinational transaction? Who is liable? For what damages? In which court?

Several discussion groups, research centers, and academic and professional groups are studying the problem. The proceedings of an international conference on Internet Law and Policy set up by a legal think tank located at the University of Washington reflect the latest developments on the subject.[7]

Meanwhile, traditional law has been applied to the Internet cases that have been brought to court. One of the key aspects of a case is to determine which courts have jurisdiction over the defendant. In most cases, the country or state where the company is established or where a person resides has jurisdiction. In practical terms, that means that a Singaporean company selling internationally through the Web can be sued only in Singapore. There are exceptions, as when you direct your marketing efforts toward one particular country; in that case, a dissatisfied customer may perhaps sue you there.

You must be especially careful if you are trading products or services that could in any way be construed as being culturally sensitive (see Cultural Diversity, below). But for the most part, the rule of thumb is to follow the laws of your own country scrupulously (even more strictly than you would if you traded only locally, if that's possible) and be very clear with your international customers about *exactly* what you are selling and *exactly* what the conditions are.

You will find more information about law and liability in the books listed in the Recommended Further Reading section at the end of the chapter.[8]

Copyright

E-commerce is offering products and services that nobody could have foreseen only five years ago. Advice, news, quizzes, entertainment, and an amazing plethora of content and information are now available in the form of text, still images, clips, sound, music, video, and interactive formats. Some of this content is free, and the producers make their money from advertisements, as do commercial radio and television stations. But some of it is protected by copyright. Copyright is the exclusive right to make and dispose of copies of a literary, musical, or artistic work—that is, the right of the creators to the sole ownership of their creation.

Copyright protection generally means that certain uses of the work are lawful only if they are done with the authorization of the owner of the copyright. The following rights are most relevant to the Internet:

· The right to copy or otherwise reproduce any kind of work;

· The right to distribute copies to the public (which is particularly pertinent on the Net);

· The right to rent copies of at least certain categories of works (such as software and audiovisual works); and

• The right to communicate performances of artistic works to the public, which will become more important as the higher speeds of broadband reach the market.

In one year, around 1 million books are published, some 5,000 feature films are produced, and around 3 billion CDs are sold worldwide. These figures are expected to grow dramatically with the proliferation of Internet access, and copyright protection will be mandatory. The growth will be due to the new availability of a distribution channel that is, at one time, cheap and accessible to anyone.

Two transactions on the Internet involving copyright are the most common:

• Online license, when the user accesses the material for a specified use and needs the authorization of the owner of the copyright; and

• Online purchase, when the owner of the copyright sets a price for the different uses of a work, and the user pays that price to have the right to use the work, sometimes also for a specified reason.[9]

Contracts may be simple and preprinted and shown to the user, who, in most cases, will only have to click on the "I agree" button of the Web site. When a payment is involved, the transaction is similar to any other sale online, and, in general, the stream of bits is delivered online immediately after the payment is processed.

The World Intellectual Property Organization (WIPO), the United Nations body that regulates copyright, has produced several international agreements on copyright and is the primary source of information on the subject.[10] If your operation involves any kind of copyright material, it is worth checking the rules to be applied in your particular case in the organization's Web site. WIPO is also working to produce an international procedure that will guarantee enforceability of the rules governing copyright, an aspect of the law that has become increasingly complex in the Internet era.

Domain Names

One area of particular interest regarding intellectual property rights (and a source of international contention) is the domain-name system for assigning Web-page addresses, which translates names into Internet protocol numbers that designate a site's particular location on the Net. *New York Times* writer on language William Safire has unofficially dubbed the Internet-naming procedure "netenclature."[11] As the Internet moved from being an academic tool to a useful business resource and from an U.S. novelty to a worldwide necessity, the need for some kind of regulation became apparent. After a bitter international dispute, a private organization called the Internet Corporation for Assigned Names and Numbers (ICANN)[12] and governed by an international counsel (representatives from all over the world) was organized, originally by the U.S. government, to deal with the issue, and the registration of domain names was thereby opened up to the private sector. When a company decides to go online, one of its first steps is to register one or more domain name(s) not only in its own country but also in the countries in which it may want to be active in the foreseeable future.

Privacy

The Internet is frequently depicted as a community. As such, it has an implied responsibility to provide its citizens with one of the most desired qualities for a community—safety.

Most large commercial sites use a technology nicknamed "cookie" to identify users and their computers. It is used to "remember" data from that particular user, such as address and credit-card information, so that the user does not have to provide it again on a return visit to the site. That is the technology's benign use.

But as consumers travel the Web from page to page, they leave footprints everywhere, and their individual preferences, choices, and other personal data may be monitored by companies that can then sell this information to other companies. Some users are actually paid for this information, which is, of course, a legal activity. Some companies use this information for statistical purposes, in an aggregate fashion, which also seems acceptable. But some companies exploit the commercial value of this data without informing users that they are unwittingly providing companies with saleable information. In some extreme instances the personal information is used against the user's explicit will.[13] So cookies can help companies track user preferences (which is sometimes helpful to the user for repeat visits) in a positive way, but they can also identify users to advertisers and other commercial interests, often without the user's knowledge or consent. This is one of the technology's questionable if not outright illegal uses.

All of this activity is connected to the principle of privacy: most users do not want information about themselves to be made available to companies without their explicit consent. The privacy issue has already been debated in the context of catalog sales. But on the Internet it has become even more immediate and crucial, given the broad and instantaneous access to such information by commercial interests. Typical users of the Internet regularly receive large amounts of junk e-mail, including sales notices, unsolicited advice on financial matters, and content related to subjects pertaining to sites that users have visited.

An important international reference document related to privacy is the OECD's "Guidelines on the Protection of Privacy and Transborder Flows of International Data," issued in 1980.[14] The European Union (EU) went further and issued a directive on privacy in 1995, which stated that the member countries had until 1998 to enact national laws to comply with the directive.[15] (Efforts by most EU countries in this regard are still under way.) One of the provisions states that members are prohibited from exporting data to a third country (non-EU) that "does not ensure an adequate level of protection." Enforcement of this article will be difficult, however: the United States, for instance, would not qualify, which will probably render some of the provisions in the directive as nonimplementable.[16]

In any case, companies doing business internationally should make every effort to protect the privacy of their users by observing the following guidelines:

• State your company's privacy policy on the homepage of your Web site.[17]

• When you ask for user input of data, explain clearly what you *are* and *are not* going to do with it.

• Treat the user's credit information with the utmost care, and consider contracting out the payment service altogether, transferring the responsibility for the data to other companies.

• Don't default a breach of privacy; make the user explicitly opt to have his or her name included on a list, not the other way round.

• State clearly what users should do if they decide to opt out of whatever list you put them on.

• Remember that in the physical world, money is anonymous; whenever possible, preserve the user's anonymity online.

• Don't "help" users by sending unsolicited e-mails (notes, releases, and advertisement) that you are not sure they want to receive.

In the long run, privacy pays. Customer loyalty will be one of the main sustainable assets for an e-commerce business after the initial excitement about Web-based transactions has died down.

Consumer Protection

Many countries have enacted specific laws on consumer protection. Any exporter should take these laws into account on a country-by-country basis. Some of the principles of these laws, however, are universal. The OECD "Guidelines for Consumer Protection in the Context of Electronic Commerce" provides basic principles that e-commerce companies should follow:[18]

• E-consumers should have at least the same protection as consumers in other forms of commerce.

• Businesses should act in accordance with fair business, advertising, and marketing practices.

• Businesses should provide clear information about themselves.

• Consumers should be able to make an informed decision about the purchase.

• Consumers should be able to identify clearly the details of the transaction.

• Consumers should be given the chance to review their shopping list before finalizing the purchase.

• Businesses should offer secure payment mechanisms and disclose the level of security of the transaction.

• Consumers should be given a fair and timely procedure for resolution of disputes.
• Businesses should protect the consumer's privacy.

Local and International Law

When entering the international marketplace, you must ensure that your product or service does not break any international laws or any national laws of the countries in which you will be doing business. For most products, this will not be a problem. But for your own peace of mind and to avoid any future disputes, check the law with your partners, your customers, and even your competitors, since they might have already performed a similar investigation. A good starting point to check for further information is the UNCTAD site.[19]

Cultural Diversity

Language

The leadership position of the United States in international trade and in the early applications of the Internet made English the standard language of communications. This was already true in the business world prior to the Internet, of course, but the new medium reinforced the trend. Today 80 percent of the nearly 1 billion Web pages in the world are written in English,[20] and the U.S. company MCI-Worldcom carries 50 percent of the world's traffic on the Net, although only 5 percent of the world's population are native English speakers. Table 4.5 lists the eight most-spoken languages in the world. The European languages that are part of the list (English, Portuguese, and Spanish) are there because of the large populations of former colonies (the United States, Brazil, and most of South America, respectively). In the Western world, English is by far the most popular second language. But what about the third? Instead of French, German, or Italian (the three most common), for practical purposes it appears that most businesspeople should be learning Chinese, Spanish, or Russian.

This holds true, of course, for your Web site's second and third languages. English is almost mandatory. But as for other alternatives, use

Table 4.5
Most Common Languages

	Language	Country	World Speakers (millions)
1	Chinese (Mandarin)	China	885
2	Spanish	Spain	332
3	English	United Kingdom	322
4	Bengali	Bangladesh	189
5	Hindi	India	182
6	Portuguese	Portugal	170
7	Russian	Russia	170
8	Japanese	Japan	125

Source: Global Reach, http://www.euromktg.com (2000).

table 4.5 to determine what makes the most sense for your business and geographic targets.

Sexual Content

Sexual customs and mores differ widely the world over. A play that constitutes a crime of indecency in one country might be performed inside a church in another. Given the various cultural responses to sexual content and the lack of restrictions on the Internet (as evidenced by the vast number of pornographic sites), the e-commerce business owner must tread carefully in this area. Thoroughly research the cultural views on sex in the countries in which you want to do business. In some regions, the mere sale of clothing and the use of models, for instance, may be considered offensive. If you visit a target country, closely observe the public environment and the local newspapers and magazines for clues to how that society regards sexuality.

All types of people, of different ages and tastes, visit the Web. Target the group you're interested in reaching, but consider others as well. Think specifically about children. If for any reason children should not visit your site, state this clearly at the entry point, and don't try to solicit their interest.

Political Considerations

The Internet is a speedy and far-reaching vehicle for information and propaganda. For political parties and groups, it is a tool of unprecedented power for communicating and spreading political views. For authoritarian regimes, it might be the perfect vehicle for spreading propaganda and controlling their citizens' whereabouts. Technology will probably preclude the exercise of such control, however, as some governments have started to realize.

Do investigate the political conditions in the countries to which you want to export, and note any areas of possible conflict. A common mistake is to extend the reach and target of your site from one country to another that appears to have the same language or culture as the first, without considering the consequences. Consider your options on an individual basis, and be sure that political considerations do not impede your business pursuits.

Capital

Lack of access to capital, through either finance or equity investment (venture capital or other), is a major obstacle to launching and maintaining international e-commerce ventures. In a survey on SMEs done by the KITE project in Europe, 64 percent of respondents identified this barrier as the most relevant for their growth and development.[21] Cultural factors, lack of infrastructure, and security problems were also mentioned as other relevant barriers.

For Internet ventures, however, the financial picture has changed somewhat in several countries. Because of the huge gains of Internet startups in the U.S. stock exchanges (even considering the wild variations that followed in 2000), many financial groups have started to pour money into Internet ventures in other countries. A cartoon in the *Boston Globe* in 1999 aptly illustrated the e-business climate at that time. In the first frame, a little boy is trying unsuccessfully to sell lemonade from a stand on the street on a summer day, with a sign that reads: "Lemonade 50 cents." In the second frame, a crowd of bankers and reporters surrounds the boy, and his sign reads "lemonade.com."

But even with this new flurry of activity targeting a few countries and regions (for example, Europe and Latin America), capital for most new small companies around the world is scarce. The venture-capital business that spurred the Internet revolution in the United States is a local phenomenon; it is uncommon in Europe or Asia.

If your company operates in an environment where capital is unavailable or too expensive (with high interest rates), your best bet is to start slowly and forge international alliances as early as possible. The money you need for your operation can probably be accessed internationally— particularly if your business focuses on the international market.

Government Policies

Taxation
Many conferences, meetings, and discussion groups around the world are addressing the taxation of electronic sales of goods and services.[22] But besides sales taxes, commercial activities on the Internet generate business profits that are taxable in the state of residence of the business owner or enterprise.

A company's residence is its place of business or, in more explicit terms, its place of management. In e-commerce, residence is sometimes difficult to determine. For instance, one of the most important questions in international taxation of e-commerce is whether the use of a Web server in a given country will cause a foreign company to be liable for income tax in that country.[23]

The OECD plays an important role in international taxation by providing a forum for discussion and coordination of international tax polices. The OECD Model Tax Convention serves as the basis for most of the tax treaties around the world. The OECD has issued a draft of its recommendations, which are generous to taxpayers. In transactions that involve countries with tax treaties that avoid double taxation, a company will be liable for income tax on business profits in a country only when it has established a permanent physical presence in that country.

The United States does not use the OECD Model Tax Convention, but most of the articles in U.S. tax treaties are similar to it.[24] The United States is trying to establish a tax system for the Internet that accomplishes the following goals:

• Simplifies the system (current sales- and use-tax systems are too complicated),

• Does not increase taxation (the system should leave the net tax burden on consumers unchanged),

• Diminishes the burden on sellers (compliance should be easier than it is today),

• Is technologically feasible (widely available software can perform tax collection), and

• Respects all the parties' rights to privacy.

Some authorities on different government levels support the creation of an Internet tax-free zone and feel that too much time and effort are being spent in trying to figure out how to tax the Internet. The prevalent understanding is that goods and services sold internationally through cyberspace are not subject to any trade duties if the delivery of the services is done online. But governments of several countries are concerned about the substantial loss of revenue resulting from this duty-free standard.

Export Incentives

One of the major hurdles for export is the Kafkaesque bureaucracy that regulates imports and exports in many countries. In a few countries, however, regulators have made serious efforts to streamline the process. In Singapore, for instance, the throughput time for the standard customs documentation, all done electronically, is measured in minutes rather than in weeks as in most other parts of the world. Customs procedures in many regions are a holdover from another era and are perhaps one of the most critical areas of improvement for any country seeking to internationalize its economy. Be aware of the customs procedures for countries with which you want to do business.

Import Barriers

Many countries have spent years maintaining significant barriers to imports (sometimes even of foreign investment). Since the dawn of economic globalization within the past few decades, however, other countries have made substantial progress in reducing traditional tariffs, licenses, and other import barriers, although tariff rates in some areas are still high.

Import licenses, which were the most significant barrier a few years ago, are now, in many countries, generally granted automatically within a few days. In other countries, however, it is still difficult to obtain an import license.

If you are dealing with sensitive goods in terms of import barriers, such as food and agricultural products, check the pertinent regulations on a country-by-country basis. The 1990s crisis in Europe concerning "mad cow" disease and genetically modified seeds are examples of the difficulties that may lie ahead.

As a rule, you must be careful about products that might be listed for special licenses, such as weapons and radioactive materials, pharmaceuticals, cosmetics, food, and medical equipment. In some countries, high-tech items such as software, hardware, and electronic equipment may also require special licenses.

Each country has the right to decide, consistent with its own mores and customs, the kinds of goods for which it will allow e-commerce transactions. But with an increasingly global economy and the advantages of bilateral trade, countries must also comply with international regulations and eventually trim their trade restrictions—perhaps by reducing the list of restricted items only to goods and services that are particularly important economically or culturally in that country or region.

International Bodies and Their Roles

United Nations Conference on Trade and Development (UNCTAD)
The United Nations Conference on Trade and Development (UNCTAD) (http://www.unctad.org) is the U.N. General Assembly's primary organization in the field of commerce and development. Its purpose is to seek better conditions for international commerce and investments and better opportunities for developing countries in view of the constant changes resulting from globalization. It promotes seminars and roundtables all over the world and has been concentrating recently in the field of e-commerce.[25]

World Trade Organization (WTO)

The World Trade Organization (WTO) (http://www.wto.org) is the only worldwide organization that deals with the global rules of commerce between nations. Since 1998 it has been concerned with the development of e-commerce and the changes that this development brings. The WTO differentiates, for the purpose of regulation, goods and services that are delivered in a physical form from those that are delivered online. The first category follows the existing rules for international commerce. But the second is complicated.[26]

Aside from the technical difficulties of such an undertaking, the organization faced a major crisis in the end of 1999 when its ministerial gathering to discuss e-commerce (among other subjects) ended in fiasco, after 50,000 unruly demonstrators in Seattle disrupted and virtually canceled the event.

World Intellectual Property Organization (WIPO)

The World Intellectual Property Organization (WIPO) (http://www.wipo.org) is the U.N. organization for the protection of intellectual property and the administration of such agreements made between member countries. Intellectual property is divided into two types—industrial property (applied to industrial inventions, drawings, and trademarks) and copyright (applied to audiovisual media, books, music, prints, photographs, and other works of art). The impact of e-commerce on intellectual property is sufficiently significant that the WIPO maintains an information site (http://ecommerce.wipo.int) about new developments and legal decisions in that area. The newly established WIPO Arbitration and Mediation Center is an Internet-based online dispute resolution system. Although it has been developed primarily for disputes involving intellectual property, its mere existence online may transform it eventually into an alternative resource for any international commercial dispute.

United Nations Commission on International Trade Law (UNCITRAL)

The United Nations Commission on International Trade Law (UNCITRAL) (http://www.uncitral.org) in 1996 proposed a Model Law on Electronic Commerce, intended to facilitate the use of electronic means of communication and storage of information, whether or not related to the Internet. The model law tries to identify, in the electronic world, the equivalents of common concepts from the paper world, such as "writing," "signature," and "original." UNCITRAL also helps countries and legislative bodies to enact this law in their jurisdiction. The organization has published a set of Uniform Rules on electronic signatures to facilitate cross-border recognition.

Organization for Economic Cooperation and Development (OECD)
The Organization for Economic Cooperation and Development (OECD) (http://www.oecd.org/subject/e_commerce) encompasses twenty-nine countries that together are responsible for two-thirds of the worldwide production of goods and services. Its objective is to promote discussions about social policies and development of the member countries. Policy discussions involve cryptography, privacy, consumer protection, and the economic impact of e-commerce. The OECD produced a document containing a thorough review of international bodies' initiatives and activities related to e-commerce[27] and is a reliable reference on international efforts in the area of e-commerce.

European Union (EU)
The European Union's (EU) (http://www.ispo.cec.be/Ecommerce) European Commission (EC) is responsible for the development of the e-commerce sector. Its role is to keep EU countries up to date in relation to the digital economy, promote innovation, and add value in the EU economy through the dissemination of e-commerce. Its Web site lists all of its activities and decisions. The EC's primary projects explore innovation, the creation of new technologies, and the development of international laws for e-commerce (see also "Privacy," above).

Group of Eight (G-8)
Since 1995, the countries that form the Group of Eight (G-8) (http://www.g7.fed.us)—the United States, the United Kingdom, France, Germany, Italy, Japan, Canada, and Russia—have acknowledged the increasingly important role played by small companies in the development of innovations and the generation of jobs. At the same time, the

G-8 has recognized the severe obstacles and the lack of opportunities that these companies face in trying to become players in the international market. It created a pilot project called Global Marketplace for SMEs to help SMEs increase their competitive advantage in international trade by reaping the benefits of the new information technologies.

Trends

The ongoing and increasing importance of e-commerce in the development of global markets prompted the UNCTAD's secretariat to coin the term *e-velopment* to describe all activities that relate to enhancing the participation of developing countries in the world economy. Rival universities Harvard and MIT in Cambridge, Massachusetts, together launched a Digital Nations initiative and an e-development conference,[28] exploring the use of new information technologies for development. As we have seen, great imbalances in Internet access and basic telecommunications infrastructure exist throughout the world, but this situation is improving in many countries. Given the speed of e-commerce penetration, can developing countries set up their infrastructure in time to take advantage of the revolution? Chapter 8 reflects further on this topic.

In this emerging market, speedy and flexible decision making about strategic changes will be crucial to the success of SMEs. We live in the age of the Internet, and the game has changed. According to Larry Carter, chief financial officer of Cisco Systems, "It's no longer about the big beating the small; it's about the fast beating the slow."[29]

Recommended Further Reading

Nelson, C. A. *Import/Export: How to Get Started in International Trade*. New York: Liberty Hall Press, 1990.

Tapscott, D. *The Digital Economy*. New York: McGraw-Hill, 1996.

Hall, G. *Surviving and Prospering in the Small-Firm Sector*. London: Routledge, 1995.

5

Case Studies: Successful Small Companies in the Global Market

If you have built castles in the air, your work need not be lost; that is where they should be. Now put the foundations under them.
—Henry David Thoreau

Introduction

In this chapter, real cases illustrate the possibilities the Internet offers to small companies as a tool for reaching new markets and for improving service in the markets where they are players already. These companies have been successful in the international market through a combination of timing, boldness, talent, and luck. They come from different parts of the world. And, when you think of it, one of them may look just like yours.

These seven companies have found success in different sectors, different stages of development, different countries, and different strategies. The countries here cover a broad cross-section of the world—one in Asia (Singapore), three in Europe (Belgium, Ireland, and Italy), and two in the Americas (Brazil and the United States). For each country, I chose a list of companies that were small, that made more than 30 percent of their revenues abroad, and that were heavy users of the new information technologies and of the Internet in particular. All the companies' officials were interviewed on location. The seven companies presented here have been selected from a careful analysis of the reports of those interviews.

Only two of the cases are pure Internet companies. The other companies were running standard businesses and managed to take full advantage of the Internet revolution. Arguably the most important factor for their success is their commitment to superb customer service as a fundamental business principle.

Methodology

The country list reflects the intention of having countries that are large and small, and in different stages of economic development. The countries on the list are no better or worse than those not on the list in terms of Internet usage. In fact, two of the countries we wanted to include—China, because of its growing importance in the IT world, and Finland, because it is the most connected country in the world—were not chosen for logistical reasons. With this caveat, here is the list of countries:

Belgium   As a small country in Europe, it has to think of exports for its economic well-being.

Brazil   This country runs a large trade deficit and wants to foster exports through programs that give direct incentives to small companies.

Ireland   The widespread availability of government incentives for small companies makes this country unique in its efforts to become a global player.

Italy   The exploding export business in its north, performed mostly by small companies, is a lesson to many companies and countries worldwide.

Singapore   It epitomizes the economic miracle of a small country thinking big in the information technologies market.

United States   It is the leading developer and user of the Internet and many other information technologies.

For each country, we studied a large number of companies and then selected at least five companies for an onsite interview.[1] The companies were selected with the following criteria in mind: they should be small companies (meaning fewer than 100 hundred employees) (see chapter 1), have significant (more than 30 percent) export operations, use the Internet intensively for their operation (particularly electronic commerce), and preferably be not directly related to computing or the Internet (users but not necessarily IT companies).

Thirty companies were preselected for the interview, their sites were analyzed, and either the author or Sergio Andrade, another researcher at Harvard, conducted the interview. We followed these interview guidelines:

• *History* How the company started, partners then and now, first ideas, first products, results over time, fears and anxieties, crises and difficult moments, growth, present line of products.

• *Company data* Products, sales data, three-year revenues, employees, customers, suppliers and vendors, offices, IT infrastructure.

• *Internet plunge* How the Internet happened in the company: first steps, decision to join, evolution over time. Situation today: use of the Internet, intranets, extranets, etc.

• *Internet business operations* How it works: inside, outside services. Marketing strategy. Visitor tracking: how many, how is it measured? Payment mechanisms. Distribution channels. Security and privacy. Trust. Virtual communities. How to retain customers? Customer support services.

• *Exports* How it started. Evolution. Funny stories. Situation today: how much, where to, how. Languages. Plus the same issues in the item above about operations.

• *Growth projections* Three-year projection, as in a business plan. Major obstacles.

• *Recommendations* Recommendations to people who are starting their own e-commerce endeavors.

• *Other topics* Other relevant items that the company spokesperson would like to add.

The interviews were conducted between 1998 and 2000 in Brussels (Belgium); Rio de Janeiro, São Paulo, and Belo Horizonte (Brazil); Dublin and Galway (Ireland); Milano and Rome (Italy); Kuala Lumpur (Malaysia); Singapore (Singapore); and Boston, Washington, D.C., and Miami (United States).

Eventually we chose six companies and one nongovernment organization:

Gifts of Course	Belgium
Smart Price	Brazil
Kennys	Ireland
Sunglasses2000	Italy
Far East Flora	Singapore
ItradeMarket	United States
PEOPLink	United States

Gifts of Course: The Right Ingredients for Success (Belgium)

Nathalie Sintobin began her business—Mandjevol, a Flemish name—in 1994. She ran a small fruit store with the help of her parents. The store sold fresh fruits and distinctive food products. The clientele tended to be regulars, and they liked their shopping experience. By using her creativity and taking care of details, Sintobin was rewarded by the market's recognition of her high-quality breakfast baskets.

The next business step was to produce fruit baskets to be ordered by phone and delivered at home. At about this time, Benny, Nathalie's brother, went to North Carolina, in the United States, to study for a master of business administration degree. In North Carolina, he got involved in consulting work on how to do business on the Internet.

Back home in Belgium, Benny and Nathalie realized that the Internet would be the natural next step for the basket business since it was already receiving orders from distant places. The original idea was to become a national service in Belgium—and that seemed very ambitious. But as soon as the site—Fruits of Course—went online, they began to receive orders from around the world. The business had to grow. Benny looked for support at Kent University. He got some advice there and made contacts with investors. Then he wrote a business plan and eventually found a good partner in the Société Culture Finance (SCF), which was interested in investing in the business as well as in learning about the operation of e-commerce ventures. SCF's parent group had a large retail chain of clothes and didn't know how to use e-commerce to foster the retail business. Instead of risking the chain's business, the opportunity to experiment with a new company was a good option. And SCF could eventually make money. For Nathalie and Benny, the timing was perfect: they were early entrants in the e-commerce market, and investors were receptive to Internet propositions.

The site was launched in fall 1998, with a limited marketing effort. The Sintobins invested $100 in a few search engines, and sent out press releases. But it worked. Investment money was brought in June 1999, and the owners sold 49 percent of the business for $1 million.

The company began with Nathalie and Benny, and now has seven employees. Extra help was hired for Christmas 1999. As the business evolved, they focused on making things right day by day.

Fruits of Course was renamed Gifts of Course, and "*of Course" was registered for a variety of domains with the intention of establishing a brand name. With money and some results to show, it began to attract more attention. On the day of our interview, Benny was conducting an internal brainstorming session about a possible partnership with a TV station. He also found an IT partner to support software development. At that time the press was also avid for Internet stories because there weren't a lot of them in Europe yet.

The company has focused on perfecting its internal operations and consolidating its brand and its business proposal. Gifts of Course deals with people's emotions and relationships. Its services are used when someone wants to please a friend, a relative, a lover, or an employee and for a variety of reasons. And customers trust Gifts of Course. They often give orders specifying only a budget ceiling and hinting what the recipient's taste is. It is then the responsibility of the company to please the customer and the recipient.

Gifts of Course stands for trust. In Belgium, a partner personally delivers the orders. The delivery charge does not currently cover the delivery cost, but it should as the business expands. One employee is capable of handling only twenty-five orders a day. For international delivery, the company relies on TNT, which has an online tracking system. But the job is not considered done when the gift is delivered to TNT. The company tracks the delivery process and informs customers when gifts are actually delivered. The process is considered completed only when the company is sure that the gift was received.

The company had already twelve orders to deliver for the Monday following the interview. But Benny's target is thirty-two orders a day to achieve the break-even point and start making money. The projection is $1 million in annual revenues within two years.

Gifts of Course values are creativity, quality, and responsible business. The company's Web site was available in May 2000 in six languages, with appropriate description of the services provided. The site can take orders from twenty-two regions (twenty individual countries), use eleven currencies, and deal with questions related to physical and legal constraints on deliveries.

Gifts of Course has used the following ingredients:

· Total quality control from suppliers, from start to finish;

· Knowledge of core production (Nathalie) and management (Benny);

· Timing and luck;

· Capital at the right time to make it happen;

· Passion and energy; and

· Hard work.

Gifts of Course (http://www.giftsofcourse.be)

Company name	**Frucon NV**
Creation date	1994
Location	Belgium
Business segment	Gifts
Internet entry	1998
Contact	Benny Sintobin
E-mail	Benny.sintobin@giftsofcourse.com

Company Data	2000	2001	2002
Number of employees	7	11	25
Revenues	$150,000	$450,000	$1 million
E-commerce revenues	60%	90%	95%
Export revenues	40%	60%	85%
To countries	United States, Europe		

Internet Strategy and Benefits
• Total quality control from suppliers
• Superb service to clients
• True global business: world segmented into 22 regions (20 countries, "rest of Europe," and "rest of the world"), 6 languages, and 11 currencies
• Repeat customers

Advice
• Have passion and energy.
• Commit to hard work.

SmartPrice: The Culture of Haggling Becomes a Business

In 1999 a group of post-graduate students in Virgílio Almeida's e-commerce course at the Federal University of Minas Gerais in Brazil decided to develop a new software tool in order to meet one of the course's assignments. It would explore the haggling culture (the prevalent method of shopping in the country) to allow students to post and shop online for used books. The seller would set three conditions for the sale: the initial asking price, the minimum price, and the decrement to be applied in the haggling process. For those unfamiliar with haggling, it works like this: the seller sets the price of the book at say, $20, the minimum price at $14, and the decrement at $2. The buyers see the asking price and make their bids. Suppose one buyer offers $12. The program would say no but would lower the price to $18. Then another buyer may offer $13. Again the program says no and lowers the price to $16. One of the buyers then increases the offer to $15 and the deal is completed. Buyers do not know the minimum price.

The tool developed by the students was up and running, and suddenly it became a success among all the students. The haggling process, besides being an effective dynamic pricing scheme, has a ludic aspect that helped make the tool very popular. The students who wrote the program and the teachers looked for an outside company that might be interested in transforming the tool into a commercial venture. Two angel investor companies became interested and the result was the new company SmartPrice (disclosure: the author is a shareholder in one of these companies). The investors named Angelo Menhem as the new CEO.

SmartPrice's first focus was to have a new version of the software tool that would be robust enough to support the full load of real time transactions. That development took six months. Then came a series of brainstorming sessions to determine what would be the perfect market to apply the new tool. The result emerged after three sessions: it would be the closeout market. Since then, the company has had an upward curve of successes. The new manager Rejane França took the helm in 2000 and led the company in its growth and opening to the international market. The first contract was with Argentina. Then came other opportunities in Latin America and a partnership with a company in the United States.

The company had seven employees near the end of 2000 and was hiring two more. Revenues for the year (the company's first) were still small at $90,000, with $12,000 from exports. Prospects for 2001 were very positive with an estimated growth rate of 300% and export revenues of one third of the total.

The main reasons for SmartPrice's success were the sophisticated software tool developed by a top-level engineering group and the guidance they received from the investment companies from the beginning. Advice to new entrepreneurs? Rejane points out that the most important definition is to be absolutely sure of what your core competence is. You should design your product and market strategy around that technology.

SmartPrice (http://www.smartprice.com.br)

Company name	SmartPrice
Creation date	1999
Location	Belo Horizonte, Brazil
Business segment	Dynamic Pricing Software
Internet entry	1999
Contact	Rejane França
E-mail	rejane@smartprice.com.br

Company Data	2000	2001	2002
Number of employees	7	12	20
Revenues	$90,000	$400,000	$2 million
E-commerce revenues	all	all	all
Export revenues	12%	30%	30%
To countries	Argentina, Chile, United States		

Internet Strategy and Benefits
• Be an Application Service Provider (ASP).
• Revenues from licensing and also from a percentage of each transaction.
• Contract out as much as possible. Concentrate on development of best software.

Advice
• Focus on core competence
• Identify target market early

Kennys: Blending the Old and the New (Ireland)

Kennys was originally established in 1940 by the Kennys, a married couple, to lend books. In the 1950s, they focused on Irish art and literature. Then in the 1960s they began selling through catalogs, exporting Irish literature to the world. In 1974, they expanded the business to include binding. It is still a family business and includes five sons and daughters of the founders and one grandson among its forty employees.

Today Kennys sells new and secondhand Irish books, maps, and prints. It also sells Irish art and does bookbinding. It is a niche business for book lovers in the Irish content market. It does not compete directly with big chain stores or the online mammoth Amazon.com.

In 1994, Kennys was contacted by Ireland On-Line, an Internet Service Provider that was looking for clients to promote its business. Kennys had an international business already, and the opportunity and the vision came together. The company designed a simple site and opened an e-mail channel with its customers. Since the beginning, the Web operation showed its value for the company's mail-order business model. The Web investment immediately paid off by reducing mailing costs and improving communication with customers. They have since improved the service provided through the Web site, fine-tuned the business model to the new medium, and expanded market reach. The Internet was a particular boost to Irish Book Parcels, a book club focused on Irish content, with clients in forty-four of the fifty states of the United States and in thirty other countries.

The Internet entry was also the beginning of a transformation in the company toward more intensive use of the computer. Almost all employees now work with computer support. Nevertheless, the personal touch has been a tradition and possibly one of the reasons for Kennys' success. Customer relationships are recognized as fundamental, even for an Internet business. Every e-mail is answered, and expert advice is given on Irish art and literature.

Kennys has been using the Internet as a broad business tool and not only as an e-commerce medium. In addition to the public site, the company uses a separate site to communicate with some institutional clients with whom they have developed long-standing relationships. Through this extranet, they export regularly to over 100 institutional clients in the United States, including the U.S. Library of Congress and various U.S. universities.

Kennys is a big bookstore with an old-fashioned look: it has an image to preserve, and that is as a seller of antique books and art. With books stacked everywhere in its three-story building, Kennys doesn't resemble a high-tech operation. But it has a 250,000-book warehouse and 1,400 regular customers (70 percent from the Web) and 60 percent of its business is for export. The computing infrastructure gives them efficiency, and the Internet provides global reach. It has a strong business with Japanese clients, for instance, for book binding work.

At the time the interview was conducted (in late 1999), the company was improving its IT infrastructure and Web site by implementing a shopping basket. As a service-based business, the company needs to focus on deploying a functional system, so delivery service has been built over time to support export.

Growth has been averaging 25 percent yearly, with a revenue stream of 40 percent from the art gallery and 60 percent from books. The U.S. business seems to be leveling off and becoming more mainstream, where they suffer from competition from major players. The Japanese market, on the other hand, is increasing fast, since it is more specialized and more appropriate to their business model.

Public relations has been an efficient tool for marketing. The company also participates in conferences and publishes its Web address wherever possible.

Kennys makes the following recommendations for small companies venturing into the Internet:

· Don't do e-commerce for the sake of doing it.
· Complement and integrate online and offline businesses.
· Pay attention to operations so that the process really works.

From its origins as a traditional business with an old-fashioned look, Kennys has fully adopted technology, blending its processes with modern electronic communication and computing systems. Kennys jumped at the opportunity for using online marketing and global reach to capture untapped markets and was able to provide highly personal services that would be impossible without the Internet. It also benefited from being an early entrant in the market: the press, avid for news about the Internet, was an important promotion channel. Success came from the convergence of several factors—the brand, close relations with clients, the opportunity, the vision, and the proper balance between a favorable image and the application of technology.

Kennys (http://www.kennys.ie)

Company name	**Kennys Book Shop and Art Galleries**
Creation date	1940
Location	Galway, Ireland
Business segment	Irish books and art, book binding
Internet entry	1994
Contact	Orla Higgins, Marketing Director
E-mail	orla@kennys.ie

Company Data	2000	2001	2002
Number of employees	40	40	42
Revenues	$3 million	$3.8 million	$4.5 million
E-commerce revenues	45%	60%	65%
Export revenues	60%	65%	65%
To countries	United States, Japan, 30 other countries		

Internet Strategy and Benefits
* Providing same personal touch through the Web as at the store
* Operations efficiency and cost reduction: extranet to institutional clients
* Improved communications and personal and expert advice to clients
* Expanded market reach
* Growth of the Irish Book Parcels, a book club

Advice
* Don't do e-commerce for the sake of doing it.
* Complement and integrate online and offline businesses.

Sunglasses2000: Expanding the Family Business on the Internet (Italy)

Massimiliano (Max) Meloni is a pioneer in the Internet: he has had access to the Internet for some fifteen years now. He dropped out of college to start an Internet business.

His family-run eyeglasses shop (Ottica Meloni) was established in Rome in 1928. He initially rejected the idea of selling glasses over the Internet as inappropriate for a business: one tries on glasses before buying them. But after failing to find anything else that might be appropriate for an operational Internet business in 1996, he decided to give it a shot anyway and started selling branded sunglasses over the Internet. He later found out that people were trying on glasses in real stores, choosing the model they wanted, and then going home to buy them directly from his company because of the better price.

He is succeeding but raising a few eyebrows. A fashion sunglass is worth much more than the value of its materials. Design and brand are being sold, and with them, status. Big fashion brand names include Giorgio Armani, Calvin Klein, Gucci, Ralph Lauren, Ray Ban, Versace, and Porsche Design. The design houses that promote these brands have a specific price policy for each country where their products are sold and license resellers to operate in a specific region. Max gets the sunglasses from his parents' brick-and-mortar store in Rome and sells them around the world using the Internet. He has a very lean and cheap operation in Rome and, since most of the brand names are Italian, a better wholesale price in Italy. Thus he can easily compete in price in the United States, for instance.

The design houses will have to adapt to this new reality, but first there is going to be some resistance. Dolce & Gabbana, one of the suppliers, stopped selling to the physical store and threatened to sue Ottica Meloni for improper use of its products. Sunglasses2000's lawyer is confident that the suppliers cannot discriminate against them and that Italian law is on their side. The protest is a distraction but only in the local Italian market. Thus far the company does not have any problems selling abroad. In the future, Max may face direct competition from his suppliers, of course.

Sunglasses2000 offers a variety of brands, and customers may select from several sources. It obeys Internet Law Number One: the customer is king. This means developing and sustaining client trust so that customers become frequent buyers. In this case, e-mails are answered within twenty-four hours, and parts are substituted at no charge. The company also supplies parts to nonclients for a small fee (the glasses are expensive, the parts are not). Clients include young people, students, techies, and the wealthy. They are 60 percent men and are mostly from California and New York. To nurture customer relationships, Max maintains a mailing list that anyone can subscribe to (and unsubscribe from), conducts regular reviews with his customers, and advertises monthly promotions.

All the operation today is for export, and 75 percent of the business comes from the United States, with clients also in South America and Europe. Revenues are almost doubling every year without any investment in advertisements. In 2000, at the level of 200 orders a month, Sunglasses2000 beat Ottica Meloni in sales.

There are only two employees at Sunglasses2000, besides Max Meloni. The company operates on the second floor of the real store with very low operating costs. The e-commerce operation uses FedEx services for delivery, and the credit-card operation is provided by Cyber Source from the United Kingdom (the service was yet not available in Italy). The Web site was initially developed at home, but then the hosting was moved to the United States. Max tried to host the site in virtual shopping malls but decided to pursue his own independent path. Sunglasses2000 established a partnership with a brick-and-mortar Fashion Mall in New York to provide customer service in one of its most important markets. The Sunglasses2000 catalog has 800 items from sixteen brands and plans to expand to 1,200 items. At the time of the interview, Max was looking for capital to invest in advertising and to stock a basic inventory so he could serve his customers faster.

Max Meloni is generating $400,000 a year of revenue with almost no investment. He has created a brand and gained experience in the business. And he has opened new perspectives for a stagnant bricks-and-mortar business. He recommends that new e-commerce operations go global, research the competition, find a good Web-site developer, and answer e-mails within twenty-four hours.

From these initial steps, much can happen. If Max is able to position his business adequately in the market restructuring that will be forced by the Internet, Sunglasses2000 can become a large international operation. He will need to monitor the strategies that the fashion houses pursue in the Internet age and also the moves of other players—suppliers and stores. But Sunglasses2000 has the advantage of being a first mover, which can help it sustain its current growth rate.

Sunglasses2000 (http://www.sunglasses2000.com)

Company name	Sunglasses2000
Creation date	1928
Location	Rome, Italy
Business segment	Fashion sunglasses
Internet entry	1996
Contact	Massimiliano Meloni
E-mail	max@sunglasses2000.com

Company Data	2000	2001	2002
Number of employees	3	5	7
Revenues	$400,000	$700,000	$1.1 million
E-commerce revenues	all	all	all
Export revenues	all	all	all
To countries	United States, Europe		

Internet Strategy and Benefits
- Leveraging the price advantage of being established in Italy
- Quality service to clients
- International operation
- Repeat customers

Advice
- Go global.
- Research your competition.

FarEastFlora: Exploring the Customer's Passion for Orchids (Singapore)

FarEastFlora was founded by three brothers in 1965, but the flowers and gifts department was launched much later, in 1978. It was mostly a catalog-based business. Today, they are importers, exporters, and wholesalers of fresh-cut flowers. Supplies come from their own farms in Malaysia and from other countries such as Holland. There is also a local retail facility for gardening that carries over 2,000 items. It is a one-stop shop for plant lovers.

The internet entry started in 1997, but the jump into the international arena occurred in June of 1999. The company now delivers all over the world. Ryan Chioh, executive director, explains that on the Internet they can update and change products as well as hold promotions regularly. In addition, they conduct e-mail marketing exercises in order to promote their products to customers. These kinds of promotions were too costly to do before, as the returns would barely cover the investment.

FarEastFlora enjoyed a good amount of cost savings by using the internet as a virtual shop. For instance, processing a customer's order on the phone takes nearly half an hour. On the internet, however, customer service staff can simply—and in their own time zone—process the orders that come in. When there is a shortage of a certain flower, for instance, they e-mail the customer and seek permission for substitutions at a discount. Customer service has won many accolades for the kind of careful attention they pay to their customers.

Ryan adopted a strategy of establishing partnerships very early in the process to avoid the high costs of marketing the brand online: users can access FarEastFlora from the local sites of LycosAsia, Yahoo!, and MSN, and also from the regional sites of ISPs Pacific Internet and SingNet. They also partnered with an online rewards company, SurfGold, who helped to increase FarEastFlora's brand awareness.

The main export markets are the United States, the United Kingdom, France, and Japan. Sales have been made in many other countries, however, and, through another partnership with international organization InterFlora, they can reach most countries in the world. Deliveries to the United States take only two to three days. The main export flower is the orchid, which holds up well to packaging and transport.

The Singapore government has launched an initiative called the "Digital Island" with the objective of exploring all the possibilities of the new technologies. This effort has had a good impact on FarEastFlora's business since it not only raised Singapore's awareness about the possibility of shopping online but also streamlined the paperwork required for exports. Exports to consumers do not need much paperwork at all, and B2B requires licenses that can be completed online very quickly.

FarEastFlora does not believe that the catalog business will disappear anytime soon. It will take some time for everyone to set used to shopping online and also for business customers to be able to place their orders directly.

The company says that they are still learning (aren't we all?) about the Internet experience. They contracted out all the development, hosting, and maintenance of the Web site (to aurica.com)—a good strategy that allowed them to concentrate their internal effort on what they do best, which is to buy, market, and deliver fresh-cut flowers. Most important, they could spend time paying careful attention to customer satisfaction. As in the Gifts of Course case, the gift is bought by someone to be delivered to someone else, usually involving feelings of love or affection. Top-notch customer service is imperative in this kind of business.

FarEastFlora (http://www.FarEastFlora.com)

Company name	**FarEastFlora Holdings Pte Ltd**
Creation date	1965
Location	Singapore
Business segment	Flowers and gifts
Internet entry	1997
Contact	Ryan Chioh, Executive Director
E-mail	ryanchioh@FarEastFlora.com

Company Data	2000	2001	2002
Number of employees	12	16	20
Revenues	$750,000	$1,100,000	$1,500,000
E-commerce revenues	25–30%	30–40%	40–45%
Export revenues	5–10%	8–12%	10–15%
To which countries	U.S., France, U.K., Japan, Australia		

Internet Strategy and Benefits
- Close link with own catalog and physical shop
- Partnership with portals, community sites, and an online rewards company
- Constant update and change of products
- Ability to hold promotions regularly
- Cost savings

Advice
- Understand thoroughly your own products and markets (not everything is saleable online).
- Watch your costs carefully, do not spend just to get your brand out.
- Be careful about giving away "free" stuff.
- If the cost of entry is not too prohibitive, give it a try.

Itrademarket: Taking the Internet to the B2B Trade in Latin America (United States)

Arturo Nava Correa, a young Mexican entrepreneur, went to the United States in 1997 to study for his master of business administration (MBA) at Harvard Business School (HBS) in Boston. Arturo says that he came to the United States like the Europeans came to America in the previous centuries: in search of new opportunities and with dreams of a bright future. At HBS he was exposed to the emerging Internet economy. Many speakers from newly formed Internet companies came to the school to share their success stories with the students and show how they launched a product that would be the next big thing on the Internet. Arturo, a former trader back home, understood very quickly the huge potential of the Internet for creating electronic marketplaces.

As his second year at HBS rolled on, Arturo realized that he stood at the beginning of what he thought was equivalent to a new industrial revolution. He would not miss the opportunity of a lifetime to become one of its pioneers. At that point he started thinking about business ideas for electronic marketplaces, and he was ready and willing to take the plunge as an entrepreneur in the new economy.

After graduating, Arturo took a job at a Latin American Internet startup, and that is when the idea hit him: Latin American companies throughout recent history have had difficulty in exporting to foreign markets, where they always faced great challenges. Through the Internet they might be able to reach larger foreign markets at a much lower cost. So the new venture would concentrate exactly there: to revolutionize international trade for Latin American companies. Arturo then decided to start working on a business plan for an electronic-marketplace company doing business-to-business international trade in the Americas.

Two months later, business plan in hand, Arturo started to look for teammates for the new company Itrademarket. The first one to join Arturo in January 2000 was Victor, also from HBS and a native Colombian; he became so enthusiastic about the idea that he left a high-salary Wall Street job to join Itrademarket. After one month of intensely pitching the plan, they finally landed their first investment of $50,000. The first business decision was to start in the trillion-dollar food market. Itradefood was set up as an international marketplace for food products. The plan was to launch other marketplaces later on.

In March 2000, Itrademarket was selected among the top sixteen Internet startups in Latin America by Latin Venture 2000. Itrademarket attracted a lot of attention from potential investors, but a significant investment of $400,000 did not materialize until the end of the month when a Mexican seed fund decided to invest in the company. At that point Itrademarket was already a development team of four professionals.

In June 2000, the first version of Itradefood was launched, and additional offices were opened in Mexico, Colombia, and Brazil. Companies in the region eager to jump into the new e-commerce world received it with great interest.

Sales are starting to flow. The company's goal is to become the one-stop shop for international trade. Itradefood, its vertical marketplace for the food industry, matches the needs of buyers and sellers, maximizes time and savings, and provides access to new products and customers, making international trade easy and convenient. It provides the following:

- Matching services (offered-price sale, reverse auctions, and auctions),
- Customer support (professionally managed transaction support),
- Logistics (deliveries arranged and tracked online),
- Online payment (secure and convenient), and
- Credit for buyers.

Itrademarket has put customer service at the top of its priorities. The Itrademarket model will migrate from just matching services to door-to-door services that include matching, logistics, payment, and credit.

Itrademarket aims to jump expected revenues of $1 million in 2000 to $4 million in the following year. The site is available in three languages (English, Spanish, and Portuguese) and is focused on the Americas. The company sees its mission as the catalyst for trade in the Americas, being able to have a large impact on the economic development of Latin America.

Itrademarket attributes its success to

· Passion and energy,

· The right mix of skills and experiences in the management team,

· Entrepreneurial spirit,

· Hard work, and

· High levels of commitment toward a common goal.

Itrademarket (http://www.itrademarket.com)

Company name	Itrademarket
Creation date	2000
Location	Miami, Florida; offices in Latin America
Business segment	Business-to-business e-commerce
Internet entry	2000
Contact	Arturo Nava Correa
E-mail	arturo@itrademarket.com

Company Data	2000	2001	2002
Number of employees	6	10	20
Revenues	$1 million	$4 million	$10 million
E-commerce revenues	100%	80%	80%
Export revenues	all	all	all
To countries	United States, Latin America		

Internet Strategy and Benefits
- Superb customer service
- Strategic partnerships
- Global access to new buyers and sellers
- One-stop shop for value-added international trade services

Advice
- Never give up.
- Have passion and belief in the business concept.
- Organize an excellent management team.

PEOPLink: An NGO of Global Reach (United States)

Daniel Salcedo was brought up half American and half Colombian and, at forth-eight, has lived in five different countries and traveled around the globe several times. He works in a suburban house next door to his own, in the outskirts of Washington, D.C. He loves the work he does, and his organization is really making a difference: PEOPLink sells, through e-commerce, crafts from all over the world and generates revenues for small poor communities in villages from Panama to Uganda and India.

Founded by Daniel Salcedo and Marijke Velzeboer, PEOPLink is a nonprofit organization that helps artisans in developing countries and remote communities around the world to sell their products over the Internet. Formed in 1995 and incorporated as a nonprofit corporation in Maryland in January 1996, it conducts business directly with producers in the developing world, eliminating intermediaries and ensuring maximum profitability for the producer.

The idea for PEOPLink came from a venture that Dan and Marijke started in 1979 called Pueblo to People. Living in Guatemala in the late 1970s, Dan worked for the United Nations, and Marijke was completing work on a Ph.D. in public health. While working on a project in the highlands of Guatemala, the young couple was impressed by well-made, sturdy palm leaf hats made by local people. They had been thinking about trying to sell some of the crafts they had seen in Guatemala to people back in the United States, and these hats seemed like an ideal starting point. The couple explained their vision to some of the villagers and agreed to discuss the venture at the next town meeting.

After much discussion and negotiation, Dan and Marijke returned to the United States with 200 dozen hats, confident that the stylish, high-quality hats would be an instant success. Unfortunately, that didn't happen. Hat shops refused to carry them, and sales at festivals and fairs were dismal. One day, Dan took a different approach. He displayed some pictures of the hat makers at work on his table at the fair. While arranging the hats, he noticed people who might otherwise ignore him, craning their necks to see the pictures. "Do you want to see how the hats are made?" he asked of the people peering at his pictures. Dan proceeded to tell the group of onlookers about the hat makers, their lives, and the process of making hats. The group was fascinated and wanted to know more. The fascination with the hat makers translated in to interest in the hats.

It was then that Dan realized that he needed to sell both the products and their context within the lives of the artisans who created them. From this basic concept, the couple went on to found Pueblo to People. This organization marketed crafts from artisans in Latin American to people in the United States through a mail-order catalog. The organization had a successful model of self-sustaining development that empowered the poor. Its annual sales grew to $3.5 million and supported 3,000 families in more than a dozen countries.

The idea for PEOPLink came while Dan was traveling throughout Haiti, Guatemala, and Peru and witnessed what he had seen in Guatemala years before: interesting handwork and an army of people between the artisans and the ultimate buyer. Given the rapid growth of Internet commerce, Dan felt that the Internet would be an excellent channel of sales for the crafts he viewed in these countries.

But PEOPLink's goal is to go beyond selling crafts to empower people in developing countries with the equipment and skills needed to participate in the new world of electronic commerce. PEOPLink achieves this by putting equipment in the artisan's hands—teaching them how to use the Internet, how to run Web pages, how to take digital pictures, and so on.

The network set up by PEOPLink now serves over 100,000 craftsmen or technical assistants around the world, in over twenty countries from Africa and Latin America, and is well on its way to the goal of self-sufficiency by 2001.

PEOPLink maintains a Web site that lists the artisans' products for sale. Typically, PEOPLink will buy items for sale in bulk so that they can be shipped to customers quickly. All the works from a variety of producers are available in the online searchable catalog. Since the products are purchased in advance of the sale to the eventual buyer, this allows the producer to buy raw materials and supplies for creating more items. PEOPLink takes a percentage of the sale, but the majority of the profit is passed along to the artisan. By eliminating intermediaries, profits are much higher to producers.

PEOPLink (http://www.peoplink.org)

Company name	PEOPLink
Creation date	1995
Location	Washington, D.C.
Business segment	E-commerce for gifts
Internet entry	1996
Contact	Daniel Salcedo
E-mail	dsalcedo@peoplink.org

Company Data	2000	2001	2002
Number of employees	10	12	12
Revenues	$700,000	$1 million	$1.5 million
E-commerce revenues	20%	40%	50%
Export revenues*	10%	20%	30%
To countries	United States, Europe, Latin America		

Internet Strategy and Benefits
* Direct contact with producers
* Small markup
* Global access to villages and poor communities
* Targeting the U.S. market of concerned people

Advice
* You can do it.
* Have passion and belief in what you do.
* Organize your own strengths.

Note: *Products are stored and sold locally.

6

"Can I Do It Too?" Prerequisites for Success and Some Common Pitfalls

Knowing is not enough; we must apply.
Willing is not enough, we must do.
—Goethe

What I hear, I forget.
What I see, I remember.
What I do, I understand.
—Confucius

What we have to learn to do,
We learn by doing.
—Aristotle

It Is Difficult, and Yes, It Is Possible

Preceding chapters covered what is at stake for small to medium-size businesses in the world of e-commerce and presented examples of a few small companies that successfully entered the international e-commerce market. Their experiences are a useful starting point for an exploration of the necessary conditions for success in the global market.

Some of these conditions for success are traditional in the sense that they are not related to the Internet or to new information technologies and techniques. Others are specific to heavy use of the Internet and e-commerce. This chapter describes the conditions needed for traditional business success and those needed for e-commerce success—and also pinpoints some of the main causes for failure and the ways to avoid them.

The task is not easy, as we have seen. But now it is possible. Create an initial checklist of how many of the necessary conditions for success you have fulfilled, and then identify opportunities and start writing your e-business plan for the international market. The messages of Goethe, Confucius, and Aristotle in the opening quotes of this chapter are clear: as Nike's famous slogan also says, "Just do it!"

Traditional Conditions for Business Success

Every e-business is a business, of course. So, many of the traditional conditions for a new business's success still hold. The company needs good management, good people, the proper finance and market focus, and the right environment.

Entrepreneurial Management

As was shown in the first chapter, successful small companies do not have to be run by entrepreneurs. Managers can also run them. But their style of management must be entrepreneurial. The person in charge must have an obsession for opportunity, be comfortable dealing with uncertainty, and have the flexibility to admit errors and command changes in strategy. It is common to see a small company succeed not with its first product but with the second or third, mostly in the same market segment. The changes in strategy among the products are crucial. Inside the company, the manager has to lead the whole team, intuit the best direction to take, and participate in all business decisions that are important for the company. The manager who is also an entrepreneur is creative, can set and meet goals, and understands on a high level the company's business environment, using this information to detect business opportunities.[1]

Entrepreneurial managers also anticipate the future. They dedicate as much time to problem-solving meetings as to strategic planning. Planning is the tool that differentiates an idea from an opportunity. When a process of strategic planning validates an idea, it may become an opportunity. The language that materializes the planning process—the business plan—has been somewhat standardized all over the world. Business plans are instruments for lessening risks. Their main beneficiaries are not investors, however, but entrepreneurs who usually learn as they consider the various aspects of developing a business plan (see An E-Business Plan, below).

People

People are the crown jewels of any business, especially small companies. Today people need to be flexible and have a desire to work—and work well—in different positions within an organization. The hiring should follow the traditional process of creating a detailed job description and interviewing several applicants.

The main area of concern is the top management team. It is common for a company to have the right products, good marketing, and increasing revenues and then, suddenly, to face difficulties. This pattern is almost always related to an inadequate top management team.[2] Often a company quickly outgrows the management talent of the founder, and he finds himself involved in tasks for which he is not prepared and sometimes does not like, such as human resources management and administration. Because he tends to avoid working on those aspects of the business and doesn't make the necessary decisions, trouble starts. By that time, it might be too late.

A top management team must be formed at the very beginning. The original team should honestly discuss what they are and are not comfortable doing. The remaining tasks should be assigned to new people at the top of the organization, well before their presence becomes crucial to the success of the company. Companies that need to contract people with Internet skills should think seriously about the possibility of finding them there, on the Internet itself, in the virtual marketplace.

Finance

This is probably the most common cause of the infant mortality of new ventures. At some point in the company's growth, a lack of financial planning may lead to a crisis that attracts all of top management's attention. This often happens at a time when this same attention is most needed elsewhere in the organization. The results are known: running for money in the middle of a crisis secures at best very expensive money or provokes a financial outcome that compromises the owner's percentage of the company; at worst, it triggers the company's deterioration and demise. When profits show up very early in the company's life, invest in the company's growth. Don't be distracted by early profits that may be ephemeral.

Financial planning involves at least three elements:

• *Realistic estimates of cash flow, with at least twelve months of visibility*   Plan to have delays in receivables and unforeseen expenses. And review your projections at least once a month.

• *Capital restructuring whenever necessary*   Again, plan ahead. If your business is growing, the initial capital structure may no longer be adequate. Don't be afraid to give away percentages of your participation to a new company. You will end up with a smaller percentage of a much bigger pie.

• *Control*   Never underestimate this basic principle. You should know where the money is going and what it is buying. Establish a control system that does not have to be very sophisticated at first, as long as all the necessary information is there. But change the control system with the company's growth, possibly at the same time as you change the capital structure of the company.

Market Niche

Not focusing on a market niche is a common mistake of many new businesses. When you start a business, you may believe that all customers will try their utmost to beat a path to your door. They won't. In a new business based on the Internet, you can easily get distracted by amazing demographics and think, "If only 5 percent of the users buy my product, I am in business." Instead, focus on the market niche you want to explore, and understand it very well. Count it. Profile it. Think of ways that will make users interested in your product or service.

A product or service designed for one particular niche market sometimes finds it way into a different market. These unexpected successes might indicate an opportunity in a market beyond your original target. Some well-known products have followed this path: a tape that was designed by 3M for industrial use later exploded in the office and home markets; the birth control pill was originally researched to help women *have* children; and the nylon fiber developed by DuPont for clothes later became the basic material for automobile tires. Even the computer was targeted initially for scientific use and not for the general public. As one of the computer industry leaders in the 1970s said, "But who will need a computer at home anyway?" So you must be prepared for changes. But the original principle still holds true: you have to focus again on this new market that you decide to explore. In the Belgian case study, Gifts of Course, the export market came as a bonus. But once that market was identified, the company went ahead with a new focus on international sales.

Right Environment

A successful company needs a good manager, good people to hire, access to the appropriate level of finance, and a well-targeted market focus. But where does it find all of these conditions? Is there a right environment for all of these conditions? Yes and no. It is much easier to open a business and meet these conditions in the places that are "the usual suspects"—in our case studies, Washington, Rome, Singapore, Brussels, and Miami. But what about the other two—a high-tech company in Belo Horizonte (Brazil) and an e-commerce venture in Galway (Ireland)? There are two conflicting trends here. The traditional places of business—like Boston and Silicon Valley in the United States or Singapore and Shanghai in Asia—are concentrating even more talent. But we are seeing new spurts of activity in very unlikely places, and the Internet is one of the enablers of this change.

Of all the conditions set out here, one is paramount for the right environment—people. You must be either in an environment where plenty of talent is available or in an environment that has a unique advantage (quality of life, good schools, and so on) to lure people to relocate there. The "soft" environment conditions—like government incentives and business climate—also need to be favorable.

Conditions for E-Business Success

All of the above traditional conditions are important for new-business success. But other characteristics are specific to these changing times, including access to global markets, keeping ahead of the learning curve, telecommunications infrastructure, ability to change and adapt quickly, and using venture capital as opposed to general finance.

Management is crucial, and some of the techniques appropriate for small companies are not taught in schools. Ironically, business schools focus on preparing students to manage departments of large firms and not their own companies. The new management skills essential for e-business success are discussed here.

Identification of Opportunities

Identifying opportunities is key for success. In fact, Timmons describes the capacity to identify opportunities as one of the main characteristics of the successful entrepreneur.[3] Opportunities are everywhere. But just which ones are the really good ones, the "killer applications"? Four out of the seven case studies discussed in chapter 5 are targeting the U.S. market (Sunglasses2000, FarEastFlora, Itrademarket, and PEOPLink). The reason is simple. As was shown in chapter 3, the majority of the buyers in the Internet's early days were in the United States. But other aspects of the opportunities in our case studies are singular. Let us revisit them. Each one of the owners had a clear understanding of the importance of the Internet for the economy. But what did they do about it?

Rejane at SmartPrice felt strongly about providing a software tool that was useful and fun at the same time. Closeout sales was a completely untapped market that SmartPrice transformed into a profitable business. Benny at Gifts of Course, the Kennys at Kennys, and Max at Sunglasses2000 incorporated the new Internet tool into existing businesses, with great success. Ryan at FarEastFlora started a new business altogether; the Internet enabled the company to display and quickly sell the beautiful but ephemeral flowers.

Arturo at Itrademarket deliberately looked for a business to operate over the Internet. The Internet was the solution. He ran after the problem. But success came from the right choice. There was a strong market demand in Latin America for the export service he organized.

And Dan at PEOPLink translated a catalog business into an Internet business. In his case, the change to e-commerce came almost too soon. Being a former computer geek himself, the Internet attracted him before the market was ready for one of its applications, e-commerce. It is as if the market needed to catch up with him.

Strong Vision and Visionaries

All the managers we talked to had in common a strong belief in what they were doing. And in the Internet era, you need this belief much more than in earlier times. Depending on the kind of business you start, it is difficult to convince your friends of its worth, let alone family, investors, and employees. It takes vision and belief in the company to convey the same idea to the workers. Think of the Gifts of Course main product: perishable fruits for the export market. How long will the fruit take to arrive at the destination? Is there any customs control over fruit in a particular country? The problems are complex enough to make many give up, but the owners didn't, and their business is thriving—in twenty regions in the world, six different languages, and eleven currencies. It takes a visionary.

Timing

The whole game on the Internet sometimes is about who is first. Whenever you think you alone are doing something for the first time in the world, be prepared to find out that someone else might be doing it too. So the question is not so much what you do—although that is still important, of course—but how quickly you implement it. Being first always pays off. Think of it like the oil industry rush in the United States. The first people who became rich were the drillers who found oil. The second group to become rich—albeit not as rich—were the drillers who did not find oil. For as soon as the news of the new riches spread throughout the country, people with deep pockets decided to get a piece of the action too. Who did they hire to conduct the business? The drillers who had failed. So they came out on top, after all. This is the situation we are seeing today. As was shown in chapter 2, burning your first Internet company can be an asset when you start a new one.

But you need to be fast. Learn and launch has become launch and learn. Since we are still living the Wild West era on the Internet today, many things on the Web are of poor quality. That doesn't mean you can slack in your concern for quality, though. It means that the market will tolerate a few errors here and there in your Web site as long as you keep improving over time. Another reason that Web sites of small companies tend to be much more interesting than those of the large ones is that small companies think of a new feature at night and push it live on the Web in the morning. Some large corporations are so worried about possible legal action being taken against them that they spend precious weeks before launching a new service or product on the Web. And even when they launch it, they come up with so many disclaimers that they discourage the buyer.

A small company that has an idea should put it on the Web immediately. Then correct it, plan more carefully, adapt quickly to the market response to the product—and do it again. Careful planning is still a necessity here. But if in doubt, do it and correct later, not the other way round, which would be the right way to do it in more stable markets.

In our case studies, Gifts of Course had an obvious advantage in being first, since many people since them have had the same idea. But they were first. Sunglasses2000 is an even more striking example since the vendors of glasses themselves might have seen the opportunity before the owner. But they didn't. When they do, Max will have already established a brand name, a customer base, and the necessary expertise in operating an online business. He can then go on and apply the same concept to other items— as he is, indeed, planning to do—or he may choose to be bought out. Both are successful alternatives for a business that started with a minimal investment.

Another interesting benefit of being first is that you may get some free public relations. The traditional media want to showcase e-commerce examples for their audience. They can provide exposure that is amazingly cheap and sometimes free—but again it is available only to those who are first.

Think Global

Rosabeth Moss Kanter defines the world-class company as the company that is managed by an entrepreneur who has advanced knowledge, business talent, and global connections.[4] These companies transform the competitiveness of the global economy into a business opportunity. The global customer has high expectations of quality and customization of a product or service. Customer service therefore becomes paramount, particularly because the number of customers for one specific product tends to be small and dispersed throughout many parts of the world.

For world-class companies, the right environment must reproduce locally world levels of performance in terms of innovation, human resources, and competition. And they must think globally all the time.

Looking back at our seven case studies, Gifts of Course is the only company that let the international market knock at its door before moving. All the other cases started *from the beginning* by thinking of the global market. For Kennys, FarEastFlora, Itrademarket, and PEOPLink, the international market was the very motivation for starting a new Internet venture.

Thinking globally improves a company's competitiveness in the local-market, as well. When you have to face international competition in other countries, you become more careful about the product quality, customer service, and different product options—things that your local customers will also be happy to have. Thus you are in a better position in your own market. The flip side of this coin is that companies from other parts of the world will be looking into your market. So it's a sound business decision to prepare for the international competition that most certainly is going to challenge you. There is nothing more satisfying than facing the competition on their own turf first and having time to prepare your company in advance for local competition from international companies.

The Internet Is Key

The literature about the Internet's successes and failures is full of examples of companies that did not do well because they opened a separate channel to try the new "media." Separating the Internet business from the rest of the company doesn't work. Successful companies understand that e-business is *the* business. In fact, as more and more associations of bricks and clicks come about, it will be difficult to distinguish an e-business from any other business. All businesses will be e-businesses once the Internet is incorporated into all companies' mainstream activities.

In the case studies in our sample, someone saw the Internet as a chance to do something interesting for the organization. The new technology opened up the chance to do something different. In the cases of SmartPrice and Itrademarket, the Internet is the very reason for their existence: had it not been for the Internet, the business would simply not exist.

Since Internet activity is key to the success of SMEs, what about your Web site? It is almost like the old story well known to soccer fans: a penalty is so important for the game (it might define the final result of the game) that it should be kicked by the club's president, not one of the players. It is the same with a Web site: it is so important to the new venture that the company's owner should manage it. In fact, some do. The site is your sales leaflet, your marketing campaign, your sales team, your customer support, your annual report, even sometimes your offline board meeting. So do pay attention to this crucial aspect of your venture online.

There are very good tools (some of them free) to collect managerial information about what your customers are doing on your site. In our case studies, this was an important area of concern of the top management.

The Entertainment Value of the Web Experience

Many Web activities are fun, and people expect the Web experience to be fun. That means that your site should be fun too. In our case studies, five out of the seven companies provide goods that relate to emotional experiences for the customer—gifts, flowers, books related to ethnic heritage, and crafts from poor regions. Even with eyeglasses, which generally are not a gift item, there is an emotional experience involved: people often laugh when they try on new glasses. So make your site fun and respect the sometimes emotional components of purchasing.

Pleasure and excitement, on the other hand, should be present on the company's internal side as well. People who work for Internet-based companies tend to be young since the technology itself is new. So the more exciting and fun your company and site are, the better your chance of keeping your people working hard and sometimes working extended hours to meet an important deadline for the company.

In our case studies, love for the product was crucial to the success of the companies. You should enjoy assembling a fruit basket artistically, anticipating the pleasure of the recipient. You should cherish your Irish traditions to be better able to market to expatriates abroad. You should love orchids before trying to sell them. In a nutshell, the whole Web experience should be pleasurable—from the company's perspective and also from the customer's.

Love Thy Customer

All companies that have some experience with the Internet report that customer care is crucial for business survival. As was shown in the case studies, some companies explored niche markets that like to group in communities (as FarEastFlora did with orchid lovers and Kennys did with Irish expatriates). You must be part of it or at least share their feelings. And remember that your competitors are just a click away. So pay attention to your content. It must fit your customers' lifestyles, aspirations, and desires—and those change a lot from one target audience to the next.

Knowledge of the Target Markets

One common mistake that companies make as they approach the Internet is to leave the subject either to the computer guy in a small company or to the information technology (IT) department in a large one. This is a bad mistake. The Internet is not an IT issue and should never be managed by IT guys. In fact, in our case studies, only one of the managers (at SmartPrice) could be called an IT specialist.

Knowledge of the target markets and how to get there is the real expertise needed. You can identify that in each one of our case studies. So if you are looking for an opportunity to get into the Internet business, don't try to copycat the latest thing that has become popular elsewhere. Identify the niche market expertise that you and your partners have, and then look for good business alternatives. In the SmartPrice case in chapter 5, the company had a software engine that used dynamic pricing[5] to control the offer of products. But it took off only after several focus sections and brainstormings with retailers who had the problem of disposing of surplus inventory. This use for the software seemed obvious after the fact but could easily have been overlooked.

Control and Flexibility

Once the business is fun, and everyone is happy, what is next? It needs control. As the owner, you have to be aware of everything that is going on in the process—from suppliers to buyers and even to end users (who might be different from the buyers, as with gifts, for instance). Gifts of Course takes care of its orders until they reach the final destination. They even survey the results with their clients. In these early days of e-commerce, the only way to make sure that everything is working fine is to check it yourself or to ask users to call you directly if something goes wrong. Depending on the size of your clientele, this may be a viable option.

You also must be flexible. In a new business, the building blocks of the processes have not yet been established. So you have to be flexible enough to accommodate unforeseen circumstances. It does not really matter if the error is on the user's side or on your side of the transaction. Be prepared to compromise on a dispute when you have to. Dissatisfied customers may cost you their whole community. And the reverse is also true. If you are able to provide users with an outstanding way out of a dispute, a complimentary letter to you may be worth many new orders. That is another example of how a small company can do better than the large ones. The small-company owner can decide on an issue immediately, without having to obtain clearance from a central office. Some large companies have already understood this and have set up their Internet ventures as separate companies to give them flexibility in dealing with customers.

Market Opportunities

Market opportunities depend on one particular period in the evolution of the technology. But some developments that will unfold over the next few years might help you decide about your best course of action. The following areas offer small companies a good chance at success.

Infrastructure

The telecommunications infrastructure for the Internet is enormous and will grow substantially. But so are the companies that will be fighting for it. The huge telecom companies are merging in an effort to become even bigger. Stay out of this. There will be opportunities at the fringes though, and you can look into those if telecom is your area of expertise.

One area that will experience rapid growth is the simple Internet access unit—in the form of personal digital assistants (PDAs), smart cellular phones, house appliances, and so on, all connected to the Internet. There are numerous opportunities here since the market is wide open at the moment. The Internet access device that we use today—the PC—is so cumbersome for this task that our descendants will laugh and make jokes about our notorious inability to simplify access, as late as the turn of the century. Think of all the paraphernalia that you have in your PC today, even if you use it just for e-mail, browsing, and text editing. We will have our revenge, though, when we can speak our commands to our watches like Dick Tracy and forget everything about today's omnipresent PC. Voice recognition is finally coming of age, and the new devices will be able to understand fairly sophisticated commands of their users. This is a hot area.

Software Enablers

The Office Suite software that was made popular by Microsoft is the basic set needed to run almost 100 percent of your office applications today. What is the equivalent of this in the coming new easy-access era of Internet use? One way to look into this is to forget the technicalities and imagine that you have a simple device that you can talk to, that knows a lot about you, and that is connected to the Internet (or some kind of successor to the Internet). There you have access to each and every single piece of information ever produced—every film, article, song, painting, and data file that was produced in or adapted to digital form over the years. What do you think you and other people will be doing with such a device? Once you have that suite of applications, what would you need in terms of software enablers? That is where a big opportunity lies in the years ahead.

Internet Companies

Pure Internet companies are those that exist only because of the Internet. In this sense, Yahoo!, for instance, is a pure Internet company, while

Amazon.com is not. Many other applications of the Internet have not yet been developed. That is where the main opportunities lie. Think of applications involving the small-change transactions that were discussed in chapter 3. Think of simpler applications that will be easy to use. Think of distance learning or other basic needs of the population. Think about the user more than the technology or anything else. This is where the opportunities are.

Internetizing an Existing Business
A survey in the United Kingdom at the end of 1998 sampled 200 fairly large manufacturing firms. They were mostly "wired" (94 percent were on the Internet, 77 percent had their own Web sites). But on the impact of the Internet, only 2 percent—four out of 200 companies—appreciated that the Internet could threaten standard ways of doing business. The top corporate officials claimed that the major threats to their businesses came from cost control, competition, and difficulty in finding new markets. Not a single one saw the connection between these problems and the Internet revolution.

Although this survey is now dated and the situation has somewhat changed, probably the largest market to be explored in the coming years is that of the traditional old-economy companies coming into the Internet. This means opportunities for consulting, training, software and hardware tools, partnerships, everything. The movement has been identified as "clicks and bricks" or "clicks and mortar." If you want to make a sure bet, this is it. Perhaps it is not so charming as other possibilities, but it offers a definitive marketing opening.

Take your pick.

An E-Business Plan

One of the things that happens when you sit down to devise a business plan for your venture is that by writing about the venture you will understand it better. Having an idea and discussing it with colleagues and relatives are merely preliminary steps to writing it down in a way that makes sense to other people. Do it. It will improve your chances of success. The document doesn't have to be long. In fact, a report that is one to three pages is quite long enough. Don't romanticize the description. Be positive but realistic. Give facts and numbers. State exactly what your chances are. Don't hide any flaws in the plan. It is very likely that an astute investor will ask you about the very problem you were trying to disguise. Describe competitors, talk about risks, and be sincere about yourself, your partners, and your real chances. The following sketch presents the basic information that you should include.

Description of the Idea

This should be one very concise paragraph. You must be able to describe the idea in a simple way so that anyone can understand it. If it takes you more than one paragraph, it may very well be that the idea is not concrete yet. Try reading it to your husband or your mother. Pay attention to their questions after you describe the idea. These questions will probably give you a hint about what is missing in the proposal. If in doubt, go to a financial site,[6] and read the site's one-paragraph description about every publicly traded company. If one paragraph is enough for you to understand what Microsoft or FreeMarket does, then it should be enough for your idea also.

Opportunity

Describe the environment in which your idea will fit and make a difference. Then say something about the situation of the company or idea at this particular point in time. Why is it different? Exactly what is the market? How does your idea fit into the existing landscape? Also, why now?

Why You?

Now that you have convinced your audience that you have a good idea, that it fits well with the environment, and that it will have an impact, the next thing to prove is that you are the best person to implement the plan. Why you? Could someone else apply the same idea once it is made public? Is it possible to patent the idea? Why are you and your partners or management team different and more capable of carrying this idea forward? What is the commitment of all the participants? Are you and your partners risking anything? What are the technical skills and expertise necessary, and how do you propose to exercise them?

Operations

How is your venture going to work? What role is each member of the top management group going to play with offices, operations, people, support services, and research? List the major costs involved for at least the first two years. Describe your Internet strategy and also how you are going to execute it.

Finance

Here is where the business plan does start to make sense—or doesn't. Estimate revenues. Compare them with your costs, and describe what you need in terms of startup money in the form of either finance or capital. Don't overestimate revenues. Be careful not to produce numbers that can be rebuked by a specialist. Remember that on the other side of the table you may find people who are at least as knowledgeable about the Internet business as you are. State explicitly in the financial plan what your stakes are and what you are putting into the business—capital or working time. Make a brief calculation of what might be the return to the investors if everything goes well. Define the exit strategy for the investors. Talk about risks.

Be very open about your prospects. However good your business plan, it is important to be open to the imponderable. Success stories have a lot to do with sheer luck. You can and should help it, working on the details of the new idea. But as we learned from the companies in the case studies, sometimes success has more to do with luck than with anything else. The managerial capacity to identify opportunities has two components—identifying a particular situation that may be favorable to your idea or company and recognizing that one beautiful day, for some reason, luck is knocking on your door.

Recommended Further Reading

Hagel, J., III, and A. Armstrong. *Net.gain*. Boston: Harvard Business School Press, 1997.

Schumacher, A. *Small Is Beautiful*. New York: HarperPerennial, 1989.

Pottruck, D., and T. Pearce. *Clicks and Mortar*. San Francisco: Jossey-Bass, 2000.

7

Setting Up a Global Small Business: A Checklist of Action Steps

On the Internet, nobody knows you are a dog.
—P. Steiner, *New Yorker* cartoon

Introduction

At this point in the book, having studied the international situation and a few case studies, you are in a better position to decide what to do about your own company. Is it ready to go international? Does it meet some or most of the conditions for success in the global marketplace set out in the previous chapter? Is the company willing to reposition itself as a world company and consider the international arena as its mainstream of business?

This chapter presents some guidelines for assessing the opportunities for international business that exist today on the Net. But when trying to make an informed final decision about whether to expand a business into the global market, companies need to recognize that nobody knows for sure what will be the best use of these new Internet applications. Companies, big and small, are sampling the waters, trying out, checking possibilities, and studying alternatives. Ignoring the subject altogether is certainly not safe: our companies, our lives, and our families will be affected by the changes.

The Internet is a wonderful tool for small companies because it tends to level the playing field for companies of any size. On the Net it is very difficult for users to figure out who and where you are and how big your

You can find an updated version of this chapter at <www.globalsme.tv>.

company is. In fact, for many kinds of businesses, size is not important. A friend once compared this phenomenon to the now common blue jeans. At one time, rich and poor teenagers wore very different clothes, but today every teenager wears the same uniform in most of the world— jeans and T-shirt—regardless of family incomes. As this chapter's opening epigraph so succinctly says about a dog pounding on the keyboard of a PC, "On the Internet, nobody knows you're a dog!"

This chapter is not a how-to recipe for going online to the international market (references are given in the text to such sources). It is a checklist of the most relevant aspects of this crucial decision for your company's future—and the opportunities that should not be missed.

The process of setting up a global business has six phases:

· Researching the business opportunity,
· Researching the customer,
· Reaching out for the customer,
· Showing your company's face online,
· Closing the deal, and
· Providing customer service, support, and maintenance.

Researching the Business Opportunity

The first phase of the process of setting up a small global company is to do some research about the business opportunity. The Internet has opened a broad search area for identifying opportunities, establishing partnerships across national borders, and directing links between small companies. Virtual companies are now possible and economically relevant and will become even more so in the future.

Identifying Opportunities

To be able to sell in any particular market, companies have had to be physically present to understand that market. With the Internet, a small company can succeed by being there virtually. Facts, figures, statistics about almost anything are available on the Net. You can get information about a region, read its newspapers, participate in its chatrooms, and even listen to its local radio and TV stations. Information may not be easy to find,[1] but at least it is there, and the search engines will surely become more accurate in the future.

Let's take an example from fashion, one from IT, and one from the service industry. Suppose you are considering selling sandals to the U.S. market. You may try several search engines with the same keywords, and find that each search engine—and sometimes two queries on the same search engine—will produce different results. I tried *sandals U.S. market* and received ten hits: four were useless (one referred to holidays in Sandals Jamaica), four referred to useful information about the U.S. market (one was a course about how to get into the U.S. market), one was about production machines, and one was about a competitor and gave useful information about models, designs, and prices. Next, you might check the weather forecasts for various regional climate reports[2] and government regulations about import tariffs from your country. Sites containing this information are all there and ready to guide you in your business decisions.

Now consider an example from the information industry. Suppose that you have a company in Southeast Asia that develops educational multimedia content for Apple computers and you are considering selling in the United Kingdom. You may go to the Apple homepage, from there to Apple-UK, and at that location find several interesting pieces of information. You will read about the U.K. market, the news of a joint venture between Apple and a local company to produce software for the educational market (which might suggest possibilities for the course you are planning to produce), and also news about a venture with Microsoft that seems to be important for the company. Intrigued by this venture, you move to your search engine again and find news about the deal—what happened, in detail, and how that deal could affect Apple and ultimately your own product.

In the services market, suppose that a Brazilian consulting company in the telecommunications field wants to find international clients. First, it would look for a nongovernmental site X that explains the Brazilian government's regulations for the recently privatized telephone operating companies. Then, it could try to place links to its own Web site on site X, since its prospective international clients are probably accessing site X from abroad and might start visiting the consulting company's site. In this way, the consulting company could start building a list of prospective clients. Visits between sites would be more likely to happen if the consulting company provided some kind of information on its site that would be relevant to international clients—like market analysis, inside information, and statistics. It could learn about each one of the prospective clients on their Web sites and then be able to produce more knowledgeable proposals to them.

Another route that could be taken by an international consulting company to learn about the high-growth telecommunications market in Brazil would be to visit the Web sites of all the relevant stakeholders in the field, many of whom present information in both Portuguese and English. It could also find other consulting companies located in Brazil that could help them access the local market.

The real worth of consulting and of information relies on trust. And trustworthiness is not guaranteed over the Net, which may explain, at least partially, why the deluge of available information has not been applied for business purposes.

A friend once had an idea of selling "invisible goldfish" in a small sealed aquarium. The aquarium would have water and items related to the sea or lakes—but no fish. The product would be sold as a fun dinner-party or office gift and would become a conversational piece: "Have you seen my invisible goldfish?" How do you research the potential market for such a product? If you do a search with the keywords *party gifts*, you will find sites that specialize in creative gifts, funny ideas, and holiday gifts.[3] To post your product in someone else's site at a very low cost, contact the administrator of each site, and negotiate to establish the link to your site, and you may very soon be in business.

These examples for the most part refer to information gathering. The opportunity itself needs to be defined by you, based on your own understanding of the market. The novelty introduced by the Internet is that your field of action is now *the whole world* and not only your neighborhood, your town, or your region.

Establishing Partnerships
An international trading company links the producer of goods and services in one country to the consumer in another country. Trading

companies operate on a large scale by focusing on one particular market segment or on major companies. They are not, in general, much help for the small companies trying to go international. Traditionally, they buy products from the producers in one country at the lowest possible price, add a considerable margin, and sell to large distributors. Distributors, in turn, add their margin and distribute to the final retailers, which, after adding their own margin, sell to consumers. In this traditional scheme, intermediaries keep large chunks of the potential profits.

With the Internet, it is possible to establish a partnership between a small company that produces something and *other small companies* that know their target markets very well. For, as pointed out by Antony Öettinger, people might think globally but they "always drink locally."[4] Small companies are closer to a small group of consumers (their employees go to the same pub, the same church, and the same bakeries). These local companies know consumers' tastes, customs, culture, and behavior and are, better than anyone else, able to make connections with them.

Suppose you have a business of organizing foreign trips for senior citizens. The way this works today is that you organize the trips with the aid of big companies (same as the trading companies above), which grab a large portion of the revenues of the operation. With the Internet, you might consider organizing the trips directly. You know that your customers like, say, warm climates, hotels with particular kinds of services, and cheap shopping. You can contact a local operator in one particular town in a foreign country (a town that you know already or that you have searched on the Net), choose the hotel from detailed pictures of the facilities, and even make a catalog of the best and cheapest items for sale in the local shops. And the reverse is also true. Local operators, knowing the tourist potential of their towns, could search the Net for companies that organize trips for senior citizens who live in the target countries where they want tourists to come from.

Another opportunity for partnerships between countries is for two or more companies to join complementary skills or product lines to sell in each other markets or even in third markets. Some of these partnerships are obvious—such as language translation, localization[5] of products for specific markets, and division of product and package manufacturing.

Others are subtler. In the software business, for instance, companies can purchase "components," pieces of software that are reusable, from anywhere in the world, work out the necessary licenses, and package them into another product, again for sale in the global market.[6] In the fashion retail market, you can establish a partnership among your company, which produces gymnastics sports clothes in Mexico, a design shop in Bali, and a retailer in California. The opportunities here are countless and can be researched and located from an office anywhere in the world, provided that good communication facilities are available.

Understanding Virtual Companies
One of the main developments spurred by the new technologies is the emergence and growth of the virtual company. Virtual companies exist: they have offices, have intelligent people working, and know their businesses very well. In general, they understand the target market segment, buy from the producers, and contract out nearly everything needed for the goods or services to reach the customer.

Electronic bookstores are a good example. They offer books to the customer online, offer a few other services on the side to help customers decide exactly what they want, and complete the sale transaction online. Then they order the books from the publisher, deliver from one of the specialized courier companies, and keep the customer informed about the processing of the transaction. These "bookstores" may not keep a single book in their own warehouses. Even if they do keep inventory to guarantee short delivery times, they can hire the space from existing warehousing companies located anywhere that is convenient for customer delivery—next door to a major hub airport, for instance.

The company is formed of a strategic team that designs the business and its development, a group of software programmers to implement the information system and its databases, and a group of computer specialists and engineers to take care of the computer servers, network routers, and telecommunication facilities. The offices have no front door and, perhaps most strikingly, *can be located anywhere*. A virtual company can be targeting a market in one specific country and be located in another where communication facilities, or computer specialists—

the company's basic supplies—are more abundant, more qualified, or less costly.

Outsourcing activities that are not the core competence of the company is a trend that is evolving: taken to the limit, outsourcing leads to the virtual company. Even if you are not interested in becoming a virtual company, consider outsourcing parts of your production or development cycle to learn where it is most competitively done, even if the actual locations are remote from your operation.

Researching the Customer

It is not possible to overemphasize the overwhelming amount of information available on the Net about pretty much anything—including your potential customers. Although finding the exact information that interests you may be time consuming, it is time well spent once you find the right sources. In the developed world and particularly in the United States, statistics are available about so many things (most of them online) that it is likely that you can find something useful if you try.

The trends in the market are important and can be checked. More and more, customers' buying decisions may be affected by current events. So an acute observer checks not only facts that are directly related to a product but also news, weather, and current events that may affect customers.[7]

Suppose you produce handcrafted dolls and you want to search your potential customers. You can go to your search engine with the initial keywords *dolls market* and learn all kinds of interesting things. Hundreds of groups of doll collectors subscribe to specialized magazines online and offline. They participate in an online market for secondhand dolls. Companies specialize in exchanging dolls.[8] Being in the doll business, you probably already know some of these things. But by searching the Web, you will learn something about your business and your potential customers that will surprise you and might give you wonderful ideas about how to proceed.

Take another example, this one from the sports field. Suppose you produce some kind of apparel (boots or accessories) for outdoor sports like biking, canoeing, hiking, mountaineering, kayaking, or rafting. You look for adventure sports in your search engine and easily hit a site that has all the demographics of the sector.[9] You will get to know the average age and typical sex of people visiting the site, how many of them own a computer at home, their probable annual income, and the different kinds of specialized societies they join. In these specialized sites that work like clubs for hobbyists, people are much more comfortable about revealing their personal data. This may be precious information for you.

Another opportunity for research is to establish permanent links with the "virtual communities" described by Hagel and Armstrong.[10] A virtual community is made up of people from many different parts of the world who share a limited set of interests and whose main form of communication is the Net. If your product interests any of these communities (and chances are that if you want to go abroad, many related communities *will* exist), you can approach them and see their reactions. You'll need to follow specific rules for that approach, however, and traditional direct marketing might not be one of them.[11] You might exchange your ideas with the coordinator of the group (some groups have coordinators, some don't), you can give the product to a prominent member of the community for a trial (if it is good, she will do the rest), or you can become a member of the community and do long-term observations before deciding how to act. One of the things you will soon find out (to many people's amazement) is that a power shift is developing from the vendors to the consumers, and members of virtual communities are proud of this achievement.

One of the most interesting groups in these communities is the group of millions of young retirees in many parts of the world. Here you have people with a lot of time to spare, a stable source of retirement income, many singular tastes, and, more often than not, a shopping habit.[12] Virtual shopping is becoming a leisure activity for many of them. This is true in the United States and also in many other countries, including developing countries. In fact, in many countries of the developing world, the average life expectancy of the population has been increasing at an even higher rate than it has in the developed world.

Most people over sixty are not used to computers, but that, of course, will change gradually as we all age. Many seniors are already taking computer classes. "Baby boomers" in the United States[13] were exposed to the PC revolution in 1981 when they were in their midthirties, young enough to feel tempted to learn how to use the new machine; now in their fifties, they will begin to retire in a few years with full knowledge of the basic tool for Internet access. Virtual communities might become their *main* interest in life, and the related markets could become huge.

According to Media Metrix, Inc., people age fifty and over who have computers use their PCs fourteen days a month on average, for more than two hours a day, which is 47 percent higher than the average for all ages. Some sites are dedicated exclusively to older people and try to bring back the idea of a small village.[14] WebTV, the company that wants to transform TV into the main Internet-access device, is targeting older people for its line of products, capitalizing on what many still see as excessive complexity in computers today.[15]

Other commercial communities have been set up that might help your international effort. VerticalNet, for instance, has set up about forty specialized sites for business-to-business relations and, in some cases, professional communities as well. These commercial ventures might be an attractive way to break into a specific industry segment.[16]

If governments are your customers, new opportunities are coming out of the present round of negotiations in the WTO (see Chapter 4). Governments will be compelled more and more to offer their tenders for purchases online and to treat international bidders fairly. The European Union has gone a step further and set the date of 2003 for 25 percent of its own purchases to be conducted online.

Reaching Out for the Customer

When you start your Web site, nobody knows you are there. It is like printing leaflets and waiting for your customers to knock on your door asking for them. But marketing on the Net can be very effective. "Is advertising in a local newspaper really the answer when for the same amount of money you can advertise yourself globally?"[17]

Market research can be inexpensive. You can find business reports, customer surveys, and comments by specialists from the comfort of your desk and at no direct costs—although the accuracy, quality, and trust-worthiness of the information cannot be guaranteed.

To build your Web presence in the best possible way and to get the customers to know about it, you will need to consider several alternatives that are available for effective Web marketing.

Building Your Independent Site

The first step in webbing your business is to plan carefully what you want to do with it. As was shown in chapter 3, first you will need to decide how electronic your commercial transaction will be. Will the Internet be used simply to help customers with their searches? Will customers be able to order online? How is payment going to be accomplished? Is your product or service deliverable online?

The next step is to define the site's architecture. If you don't feel comfortable with the subject, hire someone who does. This step is crucial for the success of the endeavor because the architecture determines how the user will access the site, navigate around it, ask for information, and so on. Ordering online is still not comfortable for most users, and they must be reassured of the quality of the product, the delivery time, the procedure for returns (a "no questions asked" return scheme within a few weeks is expected here), and the contact information in case telephone or mail contact is required.

But even if you are only at the institutional-presence stage (and this a must for any company today), it is important to produce an interesting Web site (see Showing Your Company's Face Online, below). Some statistics refer to a doubling of the number of Web pages online *every month*, so you'd better devise something worth seeing.

Once your site is up and running, a close observation of the number and nature of visits to your site (where customers come from, how they navigate through your site, what branching decisions they make) can give you an idea about what customers are interested in and provide valuable information about your business. Exploration of this important characteristic must be embedded in the site's architecture from the beginning.

The actual hosting of the site is a highly technical undertaking better left to specialized companies. Most Internet service providers (ISPs) also do hosting for the client's site, and it can also be done internationally. Some companies are installing mirrored servers in many cities around the world so that users can access your information directly, avoiding sometimes-slow international lines.[18]

The Virtual Mall
One possibility for going online is to set up shop in one of the many virtual malls (as was discussed in chapter 3). The main advantage of being in a mall (real or virtual, for that matter) is that the consumer is attracted to the place by other means, rather than just by your own efforts. The question of using one of the malls then becomes a business decision. You can first check the shopping habits of their users, their incomes, and so on. Most of the existing virtual malls will also host your "shop," which might be an interesting alternative if you are located in a country where the speed of access in the communication lines is poor.

Uplinks
One of the most important things to think about when devising the architecture of your companies' Web presence is how your customers, partners, and the public in general will reach you. Even when you are located in a virtual mall, you have to think about direct contact. On the Web network, this is called the *uplink*. To make your URL (uniform resource locator) widely known, you can use the means available on the Web itself or the traditional ones.[19] On the Web, there are the famous search engines like Alta Vista, Yahoo!, and Lycos, which continuously browse the Web and build a database from which users locate information about anything.[20] You must make sure that the search engines know you so that when users look for the product or service that you offer, the engines will find you also. Other possible electronic pointers to your business have to be researched more carefully. One of the most common is cross-reference: you have a pointer to someone's site, which in turn has a pointer back to you.

But depending on your budget, it might be important to reach your customers directly so that they know that you exist on the Web and possibly make a *bookmark* (a direct pointer) to your address. This may involve traditional marketing tricks, such as direct mailing and advertisements.

Banners

Many of the services offered on the Net today are free. This is a holdover from the days when the network was used mainly by academics who posted information on the Net as a public service. Information-content companies today have to find a way of generating money, though. Selling exposure "real estate" is one way of doing this. Like the helmet of a Formula One racer, the shirt of a tennis champion, or product images in a televised sports event, companies sell advertisement space on their most accessed pages, in general on the site's *homepage* (or first page) but also elsewhere.[21] These advertisements take the form of a banner posted on the service-company homepage and on other pages that try to attract the user to the client company's Web site. The banners vary in size and shape and are programmed to attract the attention of the user. They are normally "live" in the sense that they may blink, pop, move, or rotate. Clicking on the banner, the user moves automatically to the advertiser's Web site. When using banners to attract visitors, it is important to maintain the context in which the users were before clicking on your banner. For instance, if the banner mentions a particular product sold by your company, the pointer should take the user directly to the description of that product and not to the company's homepage. This is difficult to achieve when you post banners in many different sites, but users find it very annoying to notice that information is lost during the context switch from the original site to the new one pointed to by the banner ad.

The cost to publish these banners depends on the popularity of the Web site in which they appear. Web sites that get a few hits a day (a *hit* or a page-view composed of several hits means that someone saw the page in his or her computer) are less expensive than million-hits-a-day sites like Yahoo! (today's leader with circa 200 million page-views a day), AOL, Netscape, and Alta Vista. Note that marketing on the Net differs from marketing via catalogs or television in that users are *already interested* in a kind of product or service when they hit your page. Direct mail to selected mailing lists is somewhat comparable, but Internet users are in control and *they decide* to go to you, not the opposite.

The pricing method for banner ads is changing from the cost per *exposure* to more sophisticated methods, such as cost for a *click through* (the user sees your ad and goes to your page) or cost for a *lead* (the user actually buys something). The popular site Amazon.com pays for leads and may be a good source of revenue for popular sites: it pays between 5 and 10 percent of the customer's spending on books or other items to the site that provides the lead for the sale. Once you place the banner code from Amazon on your page, the actual payment back to you for leads is automatic.

Hundreds of companies are trying to survive solely on the revenues received from banners in their sites. *The Economist* referred jokingly to this new craze when it asked: "Is it too implausible to imagine Dollar.com—a company that sells dollar bills for 90 cents and makes money from advertising?"[22]

The Old Tools of the Trade

Nonstorefront commerce in its many forms—such as direct mail, catalogs, and order-by-phone in response to TV ads) has been around for many years and makes hundreds of billions of dollars annually. Don't abandon these tools and tricks of the trade. Brochures, leaflets, magazine and newspaper ads, and direct mail should be used to complement your electronic marketing efforts to entice users to your site. Businesses today can seldom rely on the Internet alone. A good mixture of old and new techniques, which varies from case to case, should be developed for your particular business.

Showing Your Company's Face Online

Net users expect your site to be lively, ever changing, and updated. You will lose credibility if you leave a note at the bottom of your homepage saying "Last updated on 1/1/98" or if you lack references to current developments in your field. Planning for the Web site must address its dynamic behavior: what features are going to change, how often, what content your potential visitors will find interesting.

Because this is not traditional marketing, you can mention topics that are not directly related to your products or services just to bring more information, add fun, or convey your anger at something for one particular day or week.

Local culture is an important aspect of the international trade. Target your site to the particular culture of your main customers. Do not think for a minute that your cultural behavior is somehow standard. Assume it is not, and study in detail cultural differences between your home environment and those of your users (as was discussed in chapter 4). Virtual Vineyards, an American online retailer of wines and special foods, received a complaint from a Japanese customer because he ordered one bottle of wine and it came in a two-bottle package. For an American, the package is almost irrelevant; for a Japanese, it is an important component of a prestige product.[23]

Visual Identity

The Web site is a point of sale where the client cannot use—yet—his senses of smell, taste, and touch. In some instances he can use his ears. For this reason the visual identity of the site is directly responsible for its success. The site must be nice, beautiful, or cool, but it also must adequately represent the particular field in which your products and services are offered.

Surfability

In the intricate world of the World Wide Web, users must be coached about where they are, where they have been, and what alternatives they can take from that point onward (or backward).

Another important aspect of surfability is speed of access. Your site should reside in a host that has high-speed links to the main Internet backbones—whether in your country or somewhere else. And don't bloat your site with pretty images and photographs that take minutes to appear on the user's screen. You will lose impatient surfers. If the information you want to provide is "heavy" (a typical page today should not be more than a few tens of kilobytes), try to display pages hierarchically, showing small portions of the bulk information at a time.

Interactivity

Interactivity is one area in which the Internet excels over any other media.[24] Your Web presence can be maximized by the proper use of interactivity. User participation, opinions, and impressions should be solicited. And those who do participate need feedback, so be sure to have resources available to respond to them.

Netiquette

The unwritten rules of conduct on the Net are called *netiquette*. Diversity rules on the Net, but some of the culture that originated during its academic beginnings remains.[25] Everything used to be free on the Net, in the old academic days, so give something out for free. Don't even think of starting your homepage with a *fill-in-the-form* questionnaire that identifies the visitor. Net users like the anonymity of the Web and first want to sample your information before doing anything serious about it. Let them have it their way. Surfers like to be in control. Today people know that some Net companies have to charge for their services, of course, but users need to sample the site and "taste" what you have to offer. During the site tour, they might become interested in your company and be willing to identify themselves and register for products or services information. They might even order something from you. But don't assume too much at the start of the visit.

Closing the Deal

Beyond researching a business opportunity and researching and reaching customers, you can handle business transactions today on the Net.

Payment

Various sophisticated forms of electronic payments are in use today (see chapter 3). But ease of access, tax regulations, and rules for international money flow vary from country to country. It is probably more practical for small to medium-size companies to start by thinking about credit cards or collect on delivery (COD). The international credit-card companies have branches in many countries, making it simple to establish an ongoing relationship with them. For very small companies in remote places that do not have access to a contract with a major credit-card company, the next best arrangement is to have an intermediary in a developed country facilitate the payment system. When using these intermediaries, however, payment transfer to the producer might be delayed by as much as two months. In many countries (certainly in the United States), customers have gotten used to the idea that they can return unwanted products within thirty days of purchase ("no questions asked"). For this reason, the intermediary might hold the payment until after the thirty-day "probation" time. But such returns average no more than 5 percent of the total.

Delivery

Efficient delivery companies today ship packages quickly all over the world. The main distributors of international packages are the American companies DHL Worldwide Express, FedEx, and United Parcel Service. Depending on the product, direct delivery to each customer is not always appropriate. You might have to consider temporary storage in the target country and shipment to the customers from there. The main distributors also have logistics centers that can help you handle warehousing and inventory. The expenses for shipping and handling are normally the responsibility of the buyer and added to the purchase price.

In the case of local storage in the target country, you should avoid building up too large an inventory of products—by ensuring that the product is well chosen for the country's tastes and customs and by carefully detailing the product's specifications. Doing business remotely, customers do not know what the product really looks and feels like: detailed specifications can help you avoid an avalanche of returns. It is also advisable to have insurance against transport damages. Everyone who travels internationally knows—by looking at the state of his or her luggage at the baggage claim area of international airports—that severe transport damages are common.

Table 7.1 gives you an idea of the overall costs of an international deal. These percentages are based on real exporting companies that are based in a developing country, sell their products through an inter-

Table 7.1
Division of Revenues from a Product Sold in the United States Based on Retail Price for an E-Commerce Transaction

	Percent
Producer's cost	40%
Transportation and insurance	10
Storage	5
Financial cost	5
Producer's profit	20
Intermediary	12
Marketing	5
Contingencies	3

Source: PEOPLink (2000).[26]

mediary in the United States, share a virtual mall, do local storage in the United States, and complement their sales effort by traditional direct mailing to potential customers.[26] The direct e-commerce operation eliminates a few intermediaries and therefore leave a larger percentage of the end price with the producer.

Providing Customer Service, Support, and Maintenance

The Internet is an effective tool for providing customer service, support, and maintenance (in the manufacturing industry, after- or postsales support). This activity may be crucial for a company's success and a rewarding generator of additional revenues. Customer service, according to Pearlson and Whinston, is the "non-core-business service provided by a vendor to its customers" and can be associated with either a product or a service.[27] If your customers or perhaps your distributors are on the Net, it might be possible to organize your after-sales effort totally on the Internet. The tool is ideal for overcoming language barriers and geographical distances. Here are the major customer-service activities that you can organize.

Frequently Asked Questions (FAQs)

A frequently-asked-questions (FAQ) file is a collection of questions posed by your customers over time and answers that were supplied to them.

This valuable tool relieves your company of many phone calls, since customers' problems tend to be repetitive. A query from a customer is first directed to the FAQ collection before becoming a new request.[28]

Customer Service

Customer service by telephone calls is prohibitively expensive for small companies selling abroad. A manned call center transaction costs on average $5 per call. On the Net it costs 12 cents. The company may organize a Net customer-service operation that is not live but responds to customer requests within a fixed time period—say, twelve hours. This leaves time for translations, if needed, and for work on the actual response. Time-zone differences, for instance, can be used to the company's advantage: you can promise to answer the request in a manner that leaves many of your working hours open to tackle the problem. If your company is in Singapore, for instance, and supplies to Boston (a sixteen-hour time difference), you can promise to answer any customer requests by their next business day, which leaves almost a full working day on your side.

For non–information technology companies, customer-service architecture development will probably be contracted out. For IT companies that want to develop the service in-house, software tools facilitate the work and provide all the necessary building blocks.[29] Using information technology to improve customer service was being studied even before the Internet explosion.[30] A new Internet magazine on the subject is now available, and companies that supplied tools for the old help-desk systems are now turning their attention to the Net.[31]

It is becoming more and more important for managers to devote a large proportion of their time to external customers as market share is joined by "customer share"—or relationships with loyal customers—in the company's overall marketing plan. Power has shifted from suppliers to buyers in the new age.

Special-Interest Groups (SIGs)

Depending on your product and the diversity of your clients, you might find it productive to monitor special-interest groups that use your products. For instance, if you supply orchids to the international market (see this example in chapter 5), you may have one SIG that creates exhibits, one SIG that documents new species, one SIG that creates special arrangements, and so on. General-interest groups, for instance, might be concerned with how to take care of orchids. Note that these groups are an important marketing medium, as well. But netiquette requires that you refrain from doing a direct sales pitch while at a SIG site. Instead, use your creativity to convey the appropriate message, and let the user command the action.

Technical Documentation
Some products have complex technical documentation about building schema, sophisticated maintenance procedures, legislation, and so on that is not included in the product package. This documentation might be made available on the Net on downloadable files in your server that are accessible by the users. This may also be a registered service that is available only to registered clients.

Training
Training over the Net, also called *distance education* or *distance learning*, is becoming an increasingly important educational tool. Through the use of a small camera on a company or school PC or a bigger camera in a classroom, you can train your customers to use your product, fix problems, upgrade to the next version of the product, and so on. Distance learning today is restricted by hardware availability and also by transmission-line speed and computer-server speed, even in the developed countries. But since this technology is certain to be available and widespread within the next few years, it is prudent to consider this activity in the early stages of your overall strategy for customer support.

Customer service, support, and maintenance activities must be an integral part of the company's strategy[32]—not an afterthought. These activities keep customers happy and willing to buy more products from the same company and also can be a source of substantial additional revenues related to the sale of a product or a service in almost any company. In the context of the international arena, it might very well be the decisive factor between success and failure when a small company goes international.

Next Steps

After considering all the relevant aspects of the business of going online, you are now in a better position to decide what your next step should be. If you decide to go forward, check the current version of this chapter at

www.gessb.com

where you will find useful hints and updates to this print version. Check also the books on starting an online business at the end of the chapter. They can help you with the details of the operation.[33]

For companies that are located in the developing world, *trade points* are being developed to facilitate the physical transactions of imports and exports. The original idea, devised before the Internet era, was to develop trading centers where all the activities necessary to conduct an international transaction—paperwork, taxes, finances, information about buyers and sellers, international freight and other transport companies, government clearance offices—would be conducted at the same location. UNCTAD's Trade Point program has incorporated the Internet and is now receiving and posting millions of business opportunities on its site. Trade Points exist physically in many cities around the world and are worth a visit. Check the Web to see if they might be useful to your company.

A phrase that was heard at the 1997 World Economic Forum was "We are surrounded by insurmountable opportunities." As William Thorsell pointed out, however, "There is an ominous sense that fabulous breakthroughs and revolutionary advances are upon us—but hardly anyone knows what they are, what they mean or how to make them profitable."[34]

For most small companies, the overall message here is that they, too, can share in the "insurmountable opportunities" that are available in the world of e-commerce. Going international, you will need your Web site, and it will need to be written in the English language, the Net's *lingua franca*—whether you, the French, or I like it or not. The opportunities are just too exciting to be ignored.

Recommended Further Reading

Financial Times. *Mastering Global Business.* London: Pitman, 1999.

Kautz, G. W. *Developing International Markets.* Grants Pass, OR.: Oasis Press, 1998.

Acs, Z. J., and Bernard Yeung. *Small and Medium-Sized Enterprises in the Global Economy.* Ann Arbor: University of Michigan Press, 1999.

8

What Next? A Better World?

To be small or not to be at all. That is the question. The large have no future!
—Leopold Kohr

Introduction

This is an opinionated chapter. To this point in the book, I have tried to be factual, true to the sources, scholarly. Not here. The whole purpose of this book is to raise awareness about the opportunities for small companies in the international market. That is what you read about in the preceding chapters. In this one, I convey my ideas and try to instill in you, the reader, the same hope and enthusiasm that I am feeling about the new economy. Here is where I make clear the main motivation for the book: I do indeed think that we have a good chance of transforming this place in which we live into a better world.

Economics books, in general, have described all sorts of theories about development. The focus of most studies is how to better the situation of all the abstract collective concepts of company, economy, country, and developing world. Very few focus on the person, which ultimately is the only thing that matters. Probably the most innovative thinker about development was Leopold Kohr. The titles of his books already suggest his revolutionary thrust—*Breakdown of Nations* (1957) and *Development without Aid* (1973), for instance. His work influenced a number of distinguished thinkers and popular writers, culminating with the huge success of Fritz Schumacher's *Small Is Beautiful* (1973), which became the resource book for world leaders from Kenneth Kaunda in Africa to Jimmy Carter in the United States.

This chapter was written in the spring of 2000 in the idyllic location of the American Schumacher Society in Great Barrington, in the Berkshire hills of western Massachusetts, where Schumacher's personal library is kept. I wrote under the influence of these thinkers' books, tapes, letters, and personal notes and messages.

This book owes much to *Breakdown of Nations* and *Small Is Beautiful*. The first suggests that the world would be much more peaceful if large countries were broken down into smaller units. The second advances the concept of smallness into other realms, one of them being energy production: small units, such as solar panels and windmills, would offend the environment to a much lesser degree than factory-style power plants. *Global E-Commerce Strategies for Small Businesses* makes the case that large numbers of successful small companies all over the globe will make a better world—for the individuals who work in the company, for those who buy goods and services from the small company, and for all of us.

The Small-Size Theory of Leopold Kohr

The striking theory advanced by Kohr in his early writings and then in his book *Breakdown of Nations* is that men will become aggressive and do evil once they have the power to do so unchallenged by another party, whether the family or the state. This theory extends to the country level: once a country has the critical mass to become aggressive, it will. Kohr goes on to explain the early twentieth century's wars on the same principle. According to this theory, small units, even when belligerent, cause little harm. Therefore, dividing large countries into smaller units will reduce the risk of worldwide wars. The wars that did occur would be reduced to local skirmishes and would not threaten the world with extinction—a scenario we have had to consider during the past few decades.

Kohr's theory, initially concerned with countries and wars (the book was written in 1951, when the world was still living through the aftermath of World War II) was then developed into many other realms of thinking. It was used to criticize the developed nations and their mania of grandeur in *The Overdeveloped Nations* (1977), to give advice to developing countries suggesting that they should refuse external aid in *Development Without Aid* (1973), to suggest solutions for inner-city decay in *The Inner City* (1989), and even to work for the independence of Wales from Great Britain in *Is Wales Viable?* (1971).[1]

Kohr's line of thought is amazingly consistent and powerful, expressed in his many books, articles, and lectures all over the world. One of his short stories, called "The Duke of Buen Consejo" tells the tale of a rich person who is given the title of Duke of a very poor slum called Buen Consejo (oddly enough, "good advice" in English) in San Juan, Puerto Rico (where Kohr lived for twenty years).[2] The only condition is that the Duke has to live *in* the slum with his family. He builds a palace for himself and a square paved with marble stones. Because of these changes, people realize they can make improvements in their own surroundings. It is a wonderful story that shows Kohr's wit and imagination at its best.

Small Is Beautiful and Other Followers

After absorbing Kohr's ideas, Fritz Schumacher (who befriended Kohr and described him as the person "from whom I have learned more than from anyone else") published *Small Is Beautiful* in 1973. The book influenced a whole generation of young people who, after the brutality of the Vietnam War and the long-delayed withdrawal of the defeated U.S. forces was looking for some fresh thinking about changing the world in constructive rather than destructive ways.

Schumacher notes that the trend toward centralization brought with it the idea of order, which seems good, but that decentralization brings with it the value of freedom, which is a fundamental concept and promotes diversity, a question of survival. He also noted a trend toward bigger and bigger machines that are harmful to the environment such as huge electricity dams or nuclear plants. Small-scale operations, even if they are numerous, are less likely to be harmful to the environment: being small, whatever damage they make can be easily counterbalanced by the regenerative capacity of nature itself. The other powerful concept in the book is that technological developments should be directed toward the real needs of human beings and that means addressing their small size. Schumacher carried his ideas forward into practical applications throughout the world, and became much better known than his predecessor Kohr.

Another interesting work based on ideas found in Kohr's books is Jane Jacobs's *The Economy of Cities*, a study of how cities develop.[3] She contends that the development of almost anything else halts in a city that is dominated by one or a few huge organizations. Her idea is that the development of cities depends on the creation of new work much more than the increase in production of old work. And that new work tends to be created by small companies. The more companies a city has and the more diversified they are, the better. Jacobs also confirms the idea put forward in chapter 1 of this book—that innovations produced in large organizations have difficulty in seeing the light of day since they might be contrary to the company's immediate interests or contrary to the immediate interests of the company's *management*.

Many other works about the positive aspects of smallness followed these pioneers, but decades later we still have not converted to renewable sources of energy or wholeheartedly adopted energy-savings programs, since oil is again available and affordable (apart from short periods of price hikes). But we have a new opportunity now with the Internet to realize the dream and fulfill the promises of *Small Is Beautiful*.

The Disadvantages of Large Corporations

There seems only one cause behind all forms of social misery: bigness. Oversimplified as this may seem, we shall find the idea more easily acceptable if we consider that bigness, or oversize, is much more than just a social problem. It appears to be the one and only problem permeating all creation. Wherever something is wrong, something is too big.
Leopold Kohr

"Almost every day we hear of mergers and takeovers. . . . The great majority of economists and business efficiency experts supports this trend towards vastness."[4] This sentence was published in 1973, but we read similar statements in today's newspapers. Very large corporations are merging and forming even larger corporations at an astonishing rate. Is this a movement toward business efficiency? Who benefits from it? Some mergers do involve companies in complementary sectors and result in a company that broadens the scope of activity of the two original companies. But many mergers today are horizontal, involving companies in the same sector. These mergers tend to

- Close factories and offices,
- Make large numbers of employees redundant,
- Diminish consumer options, and
- Eliminate competition and thus increase prices.

The resulting company may be more efficient and yield better profits, although mergers sometimes fall apart because of cultural differences between companies.

So employees lose their jobs, regions suffer the impact of lost tax incomes, and consumers have fewer options and pay higher prices. Who is the beneficiary then? As in crime movies, there must be a motive, right? What is it? I would like to advance one reason. Compensation for top executives in large corporations is already a scandal, and after a merger, it is even sweeter. In all mergers there is an acquirer and an acquired company, however much the former CEOs try to disguise the operation as a merger. For the CEO of the acquirer, who is now the CEO of a much larger company, compensation has to be increased, of course. For the CEO of the acquired company, a top job awaits in the resulting company and is followed by a dismissal that costs the new company dearly. This is all agreed on beforehand, of course.

So mergers in general do no good, except for those members of top management directly involved. In fact, it is possible that we will witness a reverse movement in the future. Many large companies—AT&T, for example—are trying to split some of their business lines in order to have the advantages of smaller companies.

Uniformity
"Uniformity is hell." With such an arresting introduction Fritz Schumacher started a lecture in the United States in the 1970s.[5] Had he lived today, he would be horrified at the situation in the United States. As retail chains become bigger and bigger, the user options diminish so much that the chain brand name is substituted for the name of the retail activity or service. Thus, in Massachusetts, where I live, we don't refer to a pharmacy any more; it is "Where is the nearest CVS?" Let's go the supermarket? No. "Let's go to the Star Market." Even the local café is

now "I will see you at Starbucks." Today all town centers look exactly the same. In the standardized shops, employees have no allegiance to the company or to the owner, and turn over is measured in weeks, not even in months. For those who live in small towns for the feeling of belonging to a community, the clerks and attendants everywhere change every couple of months, so nobody in these shops know you, even if you have lived in the same town for years.

Can the Internet change this? It can certainly help. Why do people open Dunkin Donuts shops instead of their own donut shops? Because everything is easy. The chain tells you what to buy and delivers the goods to the shop, it trains you in how to make donuts, and it establishes the process of how to sell donuts. With the Internet, buying materials will be easier, and so will marketing and selling. For instance, Joe's Café may e-mail its local customers in the morning telling them of the amazing dish Joe is preparing for that day's lunch. The e-mail can even be addressed only to the people that he knows appreciate lamb or a vegetarian meal—whatever he is preparing on that day. What a different and livelier world!

The backlash against the impersonal big-box chain retailers is already starting. Some communities have resisted Wal-Mart, Dunkin Donuts, and McDonald's, and in the Berkshires in Massachusetts, when I was writing this chapter, a strong local movement was working toward denying a building license to Home Depot to erect its first mega building-goods store in the region.

Abuse of Power

The contracts that are negotiated by very large corporations and by governments are worth such large amounts of money that the bidding process may become a question of life and death (some times literally) for the companies and the careers of the executives involved in the transaction. These executives often will do anything to win the contract, including dirty tricks and bribery. This is exactly what is expected of them by the business community. And society tends to be much more tolerant of the company executive who bribes a government or business employee than of the bribed official who receives the money, even though the actions are two sides of the same coin.

Political campaign finance is another arena where large corporations involve themselves in unethical transactions. As election campaigns in most countries become more and more expensive, politicians rely on "contributions" from private donors. Some companies contribute to support the political beliefs of top management, but most are buying lobbyists in the legislature or securing a place in the line for sweet deals with the government once the election is over. In the United States, campaign finance reform is the subject of quarrels during campaigns but is avoided at all costs once the election is over.

Human Resources
Top managers in large corporations don't know employees by their names, families, or opinions. Instead, they assign employees a number and refer to them collectively as "human resources." Firing is fairly easy and painless for executives. They are not firing individuals, they are cutting 20 percent of the workforce—an amorphous mass without faces.

At one time, large corporations had an implicit social contract with their workers not to fire any employee without a very good reason. That commitment to worker welfare is long gone. "Human resources" are cut back by such huge numbers that prosperous communities have been forced into bankruptcy.

Are top managers in large corporations badly intentioned, by any measure, or at least worse than the average citizen? Of course not! They are doing their jobs and in fact doing them very well, since they reached the top levels in their companies. But they report to a board whose only worry is next quarter's profit. As Schumacher has taught us: "As a result, big organizations often behave very badly, very immorally, very stupidly and inhumanely, not because the people inside them are any of these things, but simply because the organization carries the load of bigness."[6]

An interesting study conducted at the Massachusetts Institute of Technology (MIT) developed two extreme scenarios for the business environment in the twenty-first century: in one, a few extremely large corporations dominated the landscape; in the other, many small companies would do so. Although it might be argued that the study is biased toward small companies, in the scenario of a world dominated by big corporations people would lose control even over their personal lives (marriages, for instance, would have to be intra-company!). It reminds one of a doomsday film such as *The Day After*.[7]

The Advantages of Small Companies

Accountability

In a small company, everyone knows who is in charge and who is responsible for the company's destiny. The whole company celebrates good results, and the whole company laments bad results, but ultimately the boss is accountable for decisions and employees and the public know it. This is not so in a large corporation, where in-fighting sometimes gets so intense that poor results in one department may be celebrated by another department since this may mean that resources will be reallocated and managers will be repositioned on the company's management ladder.

The boss of a small company makes decisions that are good for the company in the long run when, supposedly, he or she will still be there. In a large corporation, decisions by top managers may be more related to their prospects in the company than to the actual good of the company itself, its employees, or its customer base. Top managers in large corporations move frequently from one company to another, which leads them to favor short-term results over the long-term health of the company, a time when they probably will no longer be involved with the company.

Respect for the Environment

Small companies have a direct stake in their communities. Their owners tend to remain in one location and are likely to observe environmental and local regulations of the community in which they and their family and friends live. It is difficult to imagine a small factory owner polluting the river that supplies the water for his family. As for an executive in a multi-national corporation, pollution in another country is too remote a problem to be of any immediate concern.

Distribution of Wealth

In a society dominated by large companies, wealth is concentrated in a few owners and in the companies' top management. In small companies, even when wealth is concentrated in the owners, the overall distribution is much wider since the number of owners is so large.

Flow of Ideas

Employees in large corporations complain that their proposals get lost in the big company's bureaucracy. For employees in small companies, the owner's door is at least visible if not entirely open to them.

Although they are not the norm, several large corporations have established procedures for welcoming innovations from within: 3M and Lucent, for instance, are good examples. But big corporations have been slow to recognize the Internet revolution, to the point of despair for some people within their organizations. An article in *e-bizz* magazine in 1999 epitomizes this phenomenon: a modest employee writes to the CEO of a fictional company telling him about the Internet, saying: "I may get fired because of this, but if I didn't call your attention to it, the company would go down the drain anyway, taking with it my job all the same."[8]

Happier Workers

Small companies' workers tend to be happier than their counterparts in large ones. Some of the reasons have already been referred to in other paragraphs in this section. They know that they are important to the company, and they have a better grasp of what the company is doing and what it is all about. If you think of the time that is lost in large corporations on turf wars and procedural bottlenecks, it is easy to understand employees' frustration and cynical attitudes toward work. The attitudes and conventions rampant in large corporations have led to the great success of the Dilbert comic-strip series. Scott Adams says that he didn't have to imagine much to create the series: he was actually reporting as a journalist on what he saw happening every day in the company for which he worked. Ultimately, Adams had to leave the company: his reality-based stories were just too embarrassing.

Diversity of Products and Services

In preindustrial society, producers of good and services were linked directly to consumers. Customers placed orders according to their needs for size, color, and so on. The industrial revolution changed all that personalization with the introduction of mass production and standardization. By producing large batches of standard products, manufacturers could lower prices considerably. Consumers liked the lower cost and didn't worry much about the standard designs, and loss of variety.

For many of today's consumers, standardization no longer is satisfactory. And in the massively diversified world market available on the Internet, customers will again be able to specify exactly what color, size, shape, and material they want a product to have. For clothes, for instance, they might be able to "try" them on, with the help of a computer-aided design (CAD) tool. Some of this customization will be provided by large companies, but most of it will come from small ones that will be willing to cater to the needs of a market that is the size of one: the individual customer. This movement will certainly benefit flexible smaller enterprises.[9]

Is "Successful Small Company" an Oxymoron?

Is it unavoidable that successful small companies tend to grow and eventually become large corporations? Some owners may indeed be interested in growing the company as fast as possible and reaching the Fortune 500. But some companies may decide to spin off a second company, perhaps headed by someone else from the original company. The new company remains part of the network of the original one, and cross-fertilization may bring even more profits to shareholders still in the original company. Heading a new company is an exciting incentive for employees of the original company and discourages them from taking their good ideas elsewhere.

Recipe for a Healthy Small Company

People

Hire the people you need, of course, but choose the ones you really like, the ones whose temperament and attitude match what you have determined are important for your company. Hiring is probably the most important aspect of the company's startup process, so the final selection must be done by you. Interviewing people is an investment in your most important asset. Explain to new employees your vision, your plans for the company's future, and their place in this future. Be realistic but also optimistic, since you, more than anyone else, are betting on the company's future.

Think about dividing the company's profits with your employees. This may be done through some kind of profit sharing or, for public companies, actual ownership in the company through a stock-option plan where the employee has the right to buy a certain amount of the company's shares some time in the future at a discount. Profit-sharing and stock-option plans motivate employees to work hard so that they share in the company's successes. They also provide an incentive for employees to remain longer with a company, an important consideration in growth sectors with a high demand for new employees.

Working Environment

The working environment should both look nice and give workers the tools they need to do their work. Computers, telephones, and other office equipment cost much less today than what it costs to replace a discontent worker who decides to leave. Employees are individuals with families, problems, and different needs. The best way to design and implement a good working environment for employees is simple: just ask them. And do this constantly.

Size

There is of course no standard size for a good healthy small company. Each case is different. But there are some rules that you might want to think about. For Kohr, the ideal size of a town should allow the ruler to be able to see it all from the top of the church tower. For small companies, an ideal size would allow the owner to see every employee—to know them by name and understand their function and importance to the organization. This size could be twenty people or one hundred. But when you start bumping into people in the corridor or in the coffee room that you have never seen before, then your company is too big, and it is time to think of splitting it.

Partnerships and Associations

In this interdependent world, it is always a good idea to establish partnerships at home and abroad and to join associations. The latter are more common in the United States than in other countries. In fact, if you don't like associations, you will probably find in the United States an association of people who don't like associations (Alexis de Tocqueville explained this beautifully in *Democracy in America* in 1835).[10] Belonging to associations that have meaning for your business—trade associations, small-business associations, or even social and cultural associations—will lead to an exchange of ideas that ultimately improve your product and your marketing of that product.

Focus

Your company, being small, needs a narrow market focus and perseverance. Small companies are flexible and can change direction easily. But lack of focus is especially dangerous during the startup phase of a company when an owner is full of ideas, and tries to embrace the world with short arms. Once you evaluate a new opportunity and decide to change course, focus on that new course and persevere in that direction. Study your strengths, and focus on the best possible opportunity that can be tackled by your strengths. Don't be afraid to make mistakes. Being small, you will be able to correct them in due course.

Export

Export for small to medium-size businesses is the theme of this book, and I am trying to help you to identify and benefit from your real opportunities in the international market. Thinking about exports is a healthy way to update your company so that it continues to have the right mix of products or services, even if you are targeting only a local market. If you are not looking specifically into the international market, remember that your customers more and more will be doing so. And international companies also will be looking into your local market as well.

A Better World?

As with any new technology, the Internet can be used for good or for bad. When the Internet arrived in the developed world, the average users found another way to access information that, in general, could be found in company, town, and school libraries. When a rural school in a developing country is connected to the Internet, however, teachers and pupils gain access to information that is not currently available within their communities. With international aid, some day every school, everywhere, could be connected to the Internet.

As SMEs focus on global e-commerce, diversity, a value in itself and a sometimes forgotten law of nature, is likely to increase. Products and services that small companies export will not be commodities like TVs or VCRs. Many of them will be "cultural gifts," as defined by Hazel Henderson,[11] in the sense of goods and services that help preserve the cultural aspects of communities all over the world (see the discussion of PEOPLink in chapter 5).

In this new world of communication and information, people with disabilities, seniors, immigrants, will have more opportunities to work, to exchange information, and to buy. These are interesting markets, so be aware of the opportunity from both points of view: as a buyer and as a seller. Child bearing might become more interesting for young professional women who will be able to work from home for a certain period of their lives. Several initiatives are already exploring how the new technology can be most useful for poor communities or for seniors, for instance.[12] As well-off baby boomers age in the United States, they will become a major Internet market. Seniornet, one of the sites that specializes in the needs of seniors, contends that this age group is the fastest-growing market in terms of the number of Internet users.[13]

The Internet is a speedy and far-reaching vehicle for spreading propaganda. For political parties and groups, it is a tool of unprecedented power for communicating political views. For authoritarian regimes, it might be the perfect vehicle for disseminating propaganda and controlling citizens' whereabouts. But given the enormous complexity of the Internet, control of the Net may be neither practical nor even possible. Printing presses can be smashed, and television and radio stations can be seized. But can anyone monitor every e-mail, for example, from a particular group of individuals? Which e-mail addresses would be monitored? In what parts of the world? Through which servers? Democracy is definitively a winner here.

The network becomes a place where users participate in the life of society (the *agora*) and become real citizens rather than just consumers.[14] Therefore, the network, like citizenship, must be open and accessible to all. The Internet, as a place to exercise democracy, *must* be accessible to all. And of course the new citizen has rights and responsibilities, including the duty to respect the rights of others. Virtual communities have limitations,[15] but by facilitating representation and enhancing democracy, they will make closed regimes more difficult and costly to sustain.[16]

Small cities (Schumacher set a limit of a few hundred thousand people) may become as culturally diverse as big cities are today and have no or few big-city problems. There may be less commuting.[17] It is ironic that nineteenth- and twentieth-century workers fought battles for shorter working hours and we spend those hours gained on commuting. At this point, most urban workers would gladly trade their commute hours for work hours if only they could walk home.

In traditional economic terms, the world economy will work better because we will be working toward "perfect market" in which products and services will be offered at the best price, quality, and time possible, from the point of view of the buyer.[18]

But achieving perfect markets is not the point. What counts is that people will be happier. So it is now time to rethink our organizations. As small-company owners, we now have the opportunity to position our companies where they are the most meaningful for us and our employees.

Small companies can grab a larger share of the economic pie. It is now possible. Exports and active participation in the international market are part of the solution. I sincerely hope that this book will help you find the path to financial and social rewards. The world may and will indeed be better.

Recommended Further Reading

Kohr, L. *The Breakdown of Nations.* New York: Dutton, 1978.

Schumacher, E. F. *This I Believe and Other Essays.* Totnes, Devon, UK: Resurgence, 1998.

Spinosa, C., et al. *Disclosing New Worlds.* Cambridge, MA: MIT Press, 1997.

Notes

Chapter 1

1. The AOL deal hit the market like a bomb as a major old-economy corporation was acquired by a five-year-old new-economy company.

2. See J. Naisbitt, *Global Paradox: The Bigger the World Economy, the More Powerful Its Smallest Players* (New York: Morrow, 1994).

3. V. Biagiotti and R. S. Scholar, "The European Union and Small and Medium-Sized Enterprises," Working Document W-21, Directorate General for Research, European Parliament (1997).

4. Data from the APEC Center for Technology Exchange and Training for Small and Medium Enterprises, <http://www.actetsme.org/textonly.html>.

5. From <http://www.sbs.gov/starting/indexwhatis.html> (United States) and <http://www.chuokai.or.jp/english/index.html>.

6. Small Business Administration, Office of Advocacy, "The Third Millennium: Small Business and Entrepreneurship in the Twenty-First Century" (Washington, DC: U.S. Government Printing Office, 1995), <http://www.sbaer.uca.edu/docs/publications/pub00185.txt>.

7. See, for instance, <http://www.seniornet.com>.

8. See W. Rostow, *The Stages of Economic Growth* (Cambridge: Cambridge University Press, 1960); L. Greiner, "Evolution and Revolution as Organizations Grow," *Harvard Business Review* (July–August 1972): 37; N. Churchill and V. Lewis, "The Five Stages of Growth in Small Businesses," *Harvard Business Review* (May–June, 1983): 30–40.

9. P. Sherrid, "Angels of Capitalism," *U.S. News Online*, <http://www.usnews.com/usnews/issue/971013/13ange.htm> (October 13, 1997).

10. See R. Gavron et al., *The Entrepreneurial Society* (New York: IPPR, 1998).

11. Ibid.

12. P. Drucker, *Innovation and Entrepreneurship* (New York: Harper Business, 1985).

13. J. Hyatt: "Should You Start a Business?," *Inc. Magazine's Guide to Small Business Success* (Boston: Inc., 1998), 15–20.

14. Small Business Administration, Office of Advocacy, *Exporting by Small Firms, a Report on Exporting by Firm Size* (Washington, DC: U.S. Government Printing Office, 1999).

15. P. Timmers et al., eds., *Electronic Commerce: Opening Up New Opportunities for Business* (Brussels: European Commission, DG XIII-200, 1999).

16. "Enterprises in Europe," EUROSTAT Press Office, 1998.

17. See note 9 above.

18. World Bank, *Global Economic Prospects: The World Bank Annual Report, 1997* (Washington, D.C.: World Bank, 1997).

19. J. A. Kargbo, "Business Information and the Internet in the Developing World," <http://www.firstmonday.dk> (1997).

20. Booz-Allen & Hamilton, "Electronic Commerce for SMEs," <http://www.ispo.cec.be/Ecommerce/doc2.html> (March 21, 1997).

21. See the study by AMI-USA at <http://www.ami-usa.com>.

22. Minister of State at the Department of Trade and Industry with special responsibility for small firms, e-commerce and the information society, industry, environment, and the Radiocommunications Agency. The position is occupied by Patricia Hewitt, M.P.

23. The ISI Programme in the United Kingdom: "Doing Business in the Information Society," <http://www.isi.gov.uk/isi/mitis/exec_sum.html>.

24. B. Zider, "How Venture Capital Works," *Harvard Business Review* (November–December 1998): 131–139.

25. See, for instance, "Attracting Capital to Major Companies . . . When They Are Still Small Businesses," in *Innovation and Technology Transfer* 6 (November 1997): 13–18. Also visit the trade association at <http://www.easd.com>.

26. "Venture Capitalists: A Really Big Adventure," *The Economist* (January 25, 1997): 20–22.

27. M. Cowling, "Production Functions, the Role of Managers and Entrepreneurial Scale Dichotomies: Testing the Reid," Working Paper 46, Warwick Business School (1996).

28. L. Filion, "Différence dans les système de gestion des propriétaires-dirigeants, entrepreneurs et operateurs de PME," *Canadian Journal of Administrative Sciences* 13, no. 4 (1995): 306–320.

29. See note 12 above.

30. Small Business Administration, "Exporting by Small Firms" (see note 14 above).

31. See <http://www.sba.gov>.

32. See Softex at http://www.softex.br and Northern Development Company at <http://www.energyweb.net>.

33. P. Shakeshaft, "Opportunity Sets for SMEs and Electronic Commerce," in Timmers, *Electronic Commerce* (see note 15 above).

34. See, for instance, the Web sites at <http://www.idealab.com/>, <http://www.ehatchery.com>, <http://www.divineinterventures.com>, <http://www.icubo.com.br>, and <http://www.gorillapark.com>; and P. Henig, "And Now, Econets," *Red Herring* (February 2000): 96–108.

35. There are several associations of consorzi in Italy. See, for instance, <http://www.alceservizi.it>.

36. See note 14 above.

37. For more about the project as well as other interesting references, see <http://www.ispo.cec.be/ecommerce/Welcome.html>.

38. See <http://www.grameen-info.org>.

39. See <http://www.accion.org>.

Chapter 2

1. J. M. Keynes, Biographies, <http://www.blupete.com/l.hereture/biographies>.

2. See R. W. Lucky, "Understanding Computers and Communications," in B. M. Compaine and W. H. Read, eds., *The Information Resources Policy Handbook: Research for the Information Age* (Cambridge, MA: MIT Press, 2000), 87–88.

3. "What Is Moore's Law?," <http://www.intel.com/intel/museum/25anniv/hof/moore.htm>, accessed February 12, 1999.

4. J. Padinha, "Taking PC Prices Out of the Equation," *TheStreet.Com*, <http://www.thestreet.com/comment/economics/713190.html> (February 3, 1999).

5. All data from CommerceNet/Nielsen surveys. Accessed via NUA Internet Surveys at <http://www.nua.ie/surveys/how_many_online/n_america.html> (accessed November 17, 1998) and <http://www.nua.ie/surveys/how_many_online/index.html> (accessed May 16, 2000). One could quibble over the accuracy of the user numbers, as different surveys have found different numbers of involvement. For example, the definition of "people connected" is slippery. Does it include people who have access through connections at businesses? How are multiple family members counted? Some samples define children as twelve years old or younger, others as sixteen or younger, and so on. But we can be certain that there is significant activity when we look at the number of bits transmitted (which is relatively easy to measure), the volume of commerce (someone is buying this stuff), and the number of hits that media sites and others are reporting. And everyone's measure has been rapidly growing from period to period.

6. 1996 and 1997: Internet Advertising Bureau, <http://www.iab.net. 1998: Median of fourteen estimates ranging from $839 million to $5.5 billion, NUA Analysis, <http://www.nua.ie/surveys/analysis/graphs_charts/1999graphs/us_ad_spend.html> (accessed May 11, 2000).

7. The Internet moves so fast that it is common to describe history in terms of "Internet years" or "dog years," meaning that each Internet year is equivalent to seven calendar years. See, for instance, "Large-Scale Network Caches Provide More Bandwidth for Your Money," <http://www.inktomi.com/products/traffic/tech/economics.html> (November 17, 1998).

8. U.S. Department of Commerce "The Emerging Digital Economy," (April 1998): 2, also available at <http://www.ecommerce.gov/emerging.htm>.

9. D. Carvajal, "Amazon Surge May Reflect the New Math of the Internet," *New York Times*, January 11, 1999, C1.

10. J. Carlton, "Intel's Online Orders Reach $1 Billion a Month, Contributing to Efficiency," *Wall Street Journal*, November 16, 1998, B6; Hoover's online profile of Dell, <http://www.hoovers.com> (accessed May 16, 2000).

11. E. K. Meyer, "An Unexpectedly Wider Web for the World's Newspapers," AJR News Link, <http://ajr.newslink.org/emcol10.html> (November 17, 1998).

12. Messaging Online, "Year-End 1999 Mailbox Report," pt. 5, <http://www.messagingonline.com/> (accessed May 8, 2000).

13. For a good and brief description of the Internet, see Jack Rickard, "The Internet: What Is It?," *Boardwatch Magazine's ISP Directory*, <http://boardwatch.internet.com/isp/spring99/internetarch.html> (Winter 1998–Spring 1999). Hal Varian, dean of the School of Information Management and Systems at the University of California at Berkeley, has a site with many useful links to relevant articles and other sites at <http://www.sims.berkeley.edu/resources/infoecon/>.

14. The Internet Economy Indicators, Center for Research in Electronic Commerce, University of Texas, Austin, <http://www.interindicators.com> (accessed May 15, 2000). The study was financed with a grant from Cisco Systems.

15. World Trade Organization, *Electronic Commerce and the Role of the WTO* (Geneva: WTO, 1998).

16. See <http://www.c-i-a.com/199902iu.htm>.

17. N. Wreden: "Internet Opens Markets Abroad," *Information Week* (November 16, 1998): 2ss–4ss.

18. Ernst & Young, "Internet Shopping," *Stores* (January 1998): sec. 2, available at <www.ey.com>.

19. International Telecommunications Union, *Challenges to the Network* (Geneva: ITU, 1997).

20. See <http://www.belllabs.lucent.com>.

21. M. Thompson, "Tracking the Internet Economy: One Hundred Numbers You Need to Know," <http://www.thestandard.com/metrics/> (September 13, 1999).

22. Boardwatch, *Directory of Internet Service Providers* (11th ed.) (New York: Boardwatch, 1999).

23. Center for Research in Electronic Commerce, *The Internet Economy Indictors* University of Texas, Austin, <http://www.internetindicators.com/features.html> (accessed May 14, 2000).

24. Ibid.

25. An application service provider (ASP) essentially hosts an application on a server at a central site rather than at the site of one or more local clients.

26. J. R. Laing, "The New Dr. Doom," *Barron's* (May 22, 2000): 1ff.

27. K. DeGeeter, "In Search of the Golden Egg," *Technology Investor* (June 2000): 37. Estimate is from PriceWaterhouseCoopers.

28. D. P. Hamilton and M. Mangalindan, "Reality Bites Hard as a String of Dot-Coms See Funding Dry Up," *Wall Street Journal*, May 25, 2000, 1ff.

29. "Cisco's CEO Seeks to Continue Growth as Firm's Stock Price Loses Ground," *Wall Street Journal*, June 1, 2000, Boss Talk Column, B1.

Chapter 3

1. "The New Rules of Business Online," *Information Strategy* (July–August 1997): 34–36.

2. Angus Reid Group "Global E-Commerce Takes Off," <http://www.angusreid.com> (April 2000).

3. See <http://www.idc.com>.

4. See, for instance, the McofA Web site at <http://www.McofA.com and Jupiter Communications, "Online Holidays Sales Hit $7 Billion, Consumer Satisfaction Rising" (January 13, 2000), at <http://www.jupitercommunications.com>.

5. See article in <http://abcnews.go.com/sections/tech/fredmoody/moody990105.html>.

6. Forrester Research, "B2B to Be Market by New eMarketplaces," <http://www.forrester.com> (February 7, 2000).

7. See, for instance, <http://www.emarketer.com> and <http://www.thestandard.com/research/metrics/display/0,2799,10121,00.html>.

8. See <http://www.activmedia.com>.

9. Forrester Research, "USD7 Trillion in E-commerce Revenues by 2004," <http://www.nua.ie> (April 21, 2000).

10. Booz-Allen & Hamilton, "Senior Executives Say the Internet Is Transforming Global Business—Regardless of Industry Geography," <http://www.bah.com/

press/internet_survey.html> (May 20, 1999); Prodigy Communications, at <http://www.prodigy.com>.

11. See study by AMI-USA at <http://www.ami-usa.com>.

12. Take new car retailing, for instance: someone described a car salesman as someone who is capable of laughing loudly even when in pain.

13. It is amuzing to think of a highly paid professional (say, $100 an hour) being held hostage by a mere US$30 machine.

14. See <http://www.binarycompass.com>.

15. See <http://www.doc.gov>.

16. See <http://www2.echo.lu/bonn.conference.html>.

17. U.S. President Bill Clinton's technology advisor, Ira Magaziner, dismissed the French wariness about the subject with these words: "There will be 1 billion people trading on the Internet by the year 2002. If 40 million French are not there, no one is going to notice!" (Twenty-Fifth Annual Telecommunications Policy Research Conference, Alexandria, VA, September 29, 1997).

18. G. Gilder, "The Nine-Inch Nanosecond," *Government Technology Special Edition* (September 1997): 18–23.

19. One page-view is one display of a Web page to a user. One click-through is one display of a Web page as a result of a reference (a banner ad or a textual reference) from another Web page.

20. See, for instance, the Web site at <http://miner.bol.com.br>.

21. See their Web sites at <http://www.aol.com>, <http://www.prodigy.com>, and <http://www.msn.com>.

22. J. Weiss, "Twenty Questions about E-commerce," <http://www.c/net.com> (July 8, 1997).

23. See the article at <http://www.abcnews.go.com/sections/tech/CNET/cnet_amazon990105.html>.

24. See <http://www.barnesandnoble.com>, <http://www.borders.com>, and <http://www.amazon.com>.

25. Dell Computers, "Dell Sells USD18 Million per Day Online," <http://www.nua.ie> (May 20, 1999).

26. See, for instance, <http://www.chilnet.cl/rubros/JAULAS02.HTM>, <http://www.orchidville.com>, <http://www.epicuria.com>, and <http://www.coffeenet.com>.

27. *Information Week* (September 1, 1997): 58–60.

28. See <http://www.nua.ie/surveys/?f=VS&art_id=867667005&rel=true>.

29. See <http://www.trip.com>.

30. See, for instance, <http://www.npd.com:80 and <http://www.qvc.com>.

31. See, for instance, <http://www.buysafe.com/>, <http://www.internet-plaza.com>, <http://www.shoppersadvantage.com/>, <http://www.cybershop.com>,

<http://www.netmarket.com>, <http://www.shop4.com>, and <http://www.shopping.com>.

32. For instance, *Boston Globe*, October 7, 1999; see also the IBM Web site at <http://www.ibm.com>.

33. See <http://www.netmarket.com>.

34. See <http://www.smartstore.com>.

35. See <http://www.compare.net>.

36. See <http://www.nua.ie/surveys/?f=VS&art_id=905354956&rel=true>.

37. See <http://www.allegria.co.uk/> (United Kingdom), <http://plazaone.com.sg> (Singapore), or <http://www.topshop.com.br> (Brazil).

38. D. C. Lynch and L. Lundquist, *Digital Money: The New Era of Internet Commerce* (New York: Wiley, 1995).

39. See <http://www.cybercash.com>.

40. See <http://www.firstvirtual.com>.

41. See explanation about the SET protocol in, for instance, <http://www.visa.com/cgi-bin/vee/nt/ecomm/set>.

42. See <http://www.sfnb.com> and <http://www.royalbank.com>.

43. See a description in <http://www.cybercash.com/cybercash/services/cybercoin.html>.

44. See <http://www.verisign.com>.

45. See, for instance, Digicash, at <http://www.digicash.com>.

46. See <http://www.mondex.com>.

47. See a description of the system at <http://www.visa.co/cgi-bin/vee/nt/cash/main.html?2+0>.

48. European Commission, "A Europen Initiative in Electronic Commerce," <www.ispo.cec.be/Ecommerce> (April 4, 1997).

49. In the United States alone, 113 million people (of which 59 percent are women) buy goods through nonstorefront means.

50. P. Taylor, "Businesses See IT as the Catalyst for Change," *Financial Times IT Supplement*, October 10, 1997.

51. See <http://abcnews.go.com/sections/tech/fredmoody/moody990105.html>.

52. E. M. da Costa, "Visit to Singapore and Malaysia," PIRP/Harvard Internal Report (August 1997).

53. R. Karlgaard "Up and to the Right," *Forbes ASAP* (June 4, 1998). See also "Intenet Shares: When the Buble Burst," *Economist* (January 30, 1999): 23–25.

Chapter 4

1. World Bank, *World Development Indicators 1999* (Washington, D.C.: World Bank, 1999).

2. Ibid.

3. J. Daly, "Measuring Impacts of the Internet in the Developing World," *IMP Magazine*, <http://www.cisp.org/may_99/daly/05_99daly.htm> (May 1999).

4. See, for instance, <http://www.britannica.com>, <http://www.ebay.com>, <http://www.nationalgeographic.com/mapmachine/>, and <http://www.jupiter.com>.

5. See statistics from the VISA company at <http://www.visa.com./av/press_center/digital/statistics.html>.

6. See <http://www.rsasecurity.com/news/>.

7. See <http://www.ilpf.org>.

8. See, for instance, <http://www.hewn.com>, <http://www.legalsitecheck.com/tangleweb.html>, <http://www.amcity.com/albany/stories/1998/08/03/focus4.html>, <http://www.lawnewsnet.work.com>, <http://www.ilpf.org>, <http://www.members.xoom.com/maldonado/jur.htm>, and <http://www.escm.com/new/art/jurisdiction.html>.

9. See, for instance, the cartoon sale scheme adopted by *The New Yorker* magazine at <http://www.cartoonbank.com>.

10. See <http://www.wipo.org>.

11. See W. Safire, "On Language," *New York Times Magazine*, September 4, 2000.

12. See <http://www.icann.org/>.

13. In 1999 the Internet ad company Doubleclick and the drug merchant CVS were sued for using Internet preferences without users' permission.

14. See <http://www.oecd.org>.

15. S. Feindt and I. Culpin, "Electronic Commerce and Secure Telecommunications," <http://www.ispo.cec.be/ecommerce/sme/reports.html>.

16. The state of the art in terms of practical implementation of the guidelines can be checked at OECD, "Practices to Implement the OECD Privacy Guidelines on Global Networks," OECD Document 73163, <http://www.oecd.org>.

17. For an example from a large company, see IBM, "Protecting Privacy and Securing Data," <http://www.ibm.com/ibm/publicaffairs>.

18. See <http://www.oecd.org/dsti/sti/it/>.

19. See <http://www.unctad.org>.

20. See statistics in <http://www.oclc.org/oclc/research/projects/webstats/>.

21. C. Chappell and S. Feindt, "Analysis of E-commerce Practice in SMEs," <http://www.ispo.cec.be/ecommerce/sme/reports.html> (January 1999).

22. See, for instance, T. Hoeren and V. Käbish, "Research Paper Taxation (ECLIP—Electronic Commerce Legal Issues)," <http://www.jura.uni-muenster.de/eclip/documents/deliverable_2_1_1_taxation.htm>, or Netherlands Ministry of Finance, "Taxes in a World without Distance."

23. David Hardestry, "Web Server in Another Country: Proposed Rules," <http://ecommercetax.com>.

24. See, for instance, D. Hardestry, "Tax Plans: Final Criteria" or "E-Commerce Commission Calls for a New System," <http://ecommercetax.com>.

25. See, for instance, the results of seminars held in Caracas, Venezuela; Lima, Peru; Nairobi, Kenya; and Colombo, Sri-Lanka, at <http://www.unctad.org/ecommerce/ecommerce.html>.

26. Follow the discussions within the WTO at <http://www.wto.org/wto/ecom/ecom.htm>.

27. OECD, Directorate for Science, Technology, and Industry, *Revised Report on International and Regional Bodies: Activities and Initiatives in Electronic Commerce,* <http://www.oecd.org/dsti/sti/it/ec/act/paris_ec/index.htm> (Paris: OECD, 1999).

28. See the digital nations initiative at <http://www.digitalnations.medialab.mit.edu>, and the conference proceedings at <http://www.cid.ksg.harvard.edu>.

29. Larry Carter, at E-Commerce 2000, Boston.

Chapter 5

1. For the selection process, I had the support of the following people and institutions:
• Project Knowledge and Information Transfer on Electronic Commerce (KITE) keeps an inventory of e-commerce sites of small and medium-size enterprises within the European Union. It produces analysis and a best-practices guide, <http://kite.tsa.de>.
• Frank Roche, Dublin.
• The Giuseppe e Simone Monforte Consorzio per l'Internazionalizzazione Sviluppo e Formazione dele Inprese supports Italian enterprises in the phases of development and internationalization, <http://www.venturanet.it/apce/cisfiEn.html>.
• The Massachusetts Electronic Commerce Association promotes the electronic commerce industry in New England, <http://www.ebuzz.org/>.
• The Softex Society manages the Brazilian Software Export Program (SOFTEX 2000) and fosters the export of software, <http://www.softex.br/>.

Chapter 6

1. L. Filion, "Visions and Relations: Elements for an Entrepreneurial Metamodel," *International Small Business Journal* 9, no. 2 (January 1991): 26–40.

2. See P. Drucker, *Innovation and Entrepreneurship* (New York: Harper Business, 1986), chap. 15.

3. J. A. Timmons, *New Venture Creation* (4th ed.) (Homewood, IL: Irwin, 1994).

4. R. M. Kanter, *World Class* (New York: Simon and Schuster, 1995).

5. See company's site at <http://www.smartprice.com.br>.

6. See, for instance, <http://www.thestreet.com>.

Chapter 7

1. Someone has told me that while searching the Web to find the date of the Battle of Trafalgar he found Nelson's biography, a picture of a well-known square in London, and a third-grade essay about a school visit to London.

2. See, for instance, <http://www.weather.com>.

3. See, for instance, creative gifts at <http://www.flaxart.com>, funny ideas at <http://skansen.webalog.com>, and holiday gifts at <http://vine-n-roses.com>.

4. See A. Öettinger, "Context for Decisions: Global and Local Information Technology Issues," Incidental Paper, PIRP/Harvard University (January 1998).

5. Localization is more than the simple translation of manuals and brochures: it is the full adaptation of a product or service to the local characteristics of a particular country, including language, culture, religion, local states, and business practices.

6. See, for instance, <http://www.software.net/dist.htm>.

7. For instance, when Michael Jordan announced in 1995 that he was considering a return to professional basketball, the stock market price of the companies he made advertisements for went up $2 billion.

8. See, for instance, doll collectors at <http://www.auntie.com>, secondhand dolls at <www.1earth.com.au>, and doll exchanges at <http://www.dollexchange.com/servfaq.html>.

9. If you fancy this topic, see <http://www.adventuresports.com>, a site that claims half a million hits a month.

10. J. Hagel III and A. G. Armstrong, *net.gain* (Boston: HBS Press, 1997).

11. Direct marketing is, for most Internet surfers, had netiquette. It seldom works.

12. Even back in 1997, 24 percent of online shoppers were over age fifty-five, according to the "Matrix Directory Services," *Nielsen Media Research* (1997).

13. Those born in the United States in the high-fertility period following World War II are called *baby boomers*. The U.S. president from 1992 to 2000, Bill Clinton, for instance, is a baby boomer.

14. See, for instance, <http://www.thirdage.com>.

15. E. M. da Costa, "Y2K: Waiting for Godot," *Agrosoft Magazine* (November 1999): 16–21.

16. See <http://www.verticalnet.com>.

17. ISI (Information Society Initiative), "Doing Business in the Information Society," <http://www.isi.gov.uk/>.

18. See, for instance, Digital Island's service at <http://www.digisle.com/>.

19. URLs are Internet addresses that generally start with "http://www," a clear indication of how misguided computer wizards can be. Radio and television announcers must recite the awkward "double-you, double-you, double-you, dot" only because someone in a computer lab long ago decided on this cumbersome address system.

20. See <http://www.altavista.com>, <http://www.yahoo.com>, and <http://www.lycos.com>.

21. Unlike a print catalog, the Net sites have no rigid page hierarchy, and pages may be accessed in any order depending on internal links set up by each Web site and also on the user's interest.

22. "Internet Shares—When the Bubble Burst," *The Economist* (January 30, 1999): 23–25.

23. See <http://www.virtualvin.com>.

24. Many people think that television already is interactive. Perhaps because television shows familiar places and faces, we tend to think that we are in those place and not that they are being shown where we are. This illusion is one reason that people who meet TV personalities on the streets tend to greet them as old acquaintances.

25. Mailing lists have their own rules and can differ substantially. See, for instance, <http://www.ii.uib.no/~kjartan/aikidofaq/e_section02.html>.

26. See <http://www.peoplink.org>.

27. K. Pearlson and A. Whinston, "Customer Support Issues for the Twenty-First Century," <http://cism.bus.utexas.edu/ravi/keri.html> (November 1993).

28. See FAQs for the software industry at <http://www.marimba.com> and for the retail industry at <http://www.jcpenny.com>.

29. See, for instance, <http://inet-sciences.com/index.html>.

30. B. Ives and R. Mason, "Can Information Technology Revitalize Your Customer Service?," *Academy of Management Executive* 4, no. 4 (1990): 55–69.

31. See <http://www.csr.co.za/sample/frontpage.htm>. For an interesting example, see <http://www.aim-helpdesk.com>.

32. For an interesting example, see <http://www.aim-helpdesk.com>.

33. See also, P. Hise, *Growing Your Business On Line* (New York: Holt, 1996).

34. Reported by William Thorsell in *Globe and Mail*, August 2, 1997.

Chapter 8

1. Leopold Kohr's brilliant work can be found in the following books: *The Breakdown of Nations* (New York: Dutton, 1978); *Development without Aid: The Translucent Society* (Wales: Davies, 1973); *The Inner City: From Mud to Marble* (Wales: Y Lolfa Cyf, 1989); *Is Wales Viable?* (Wales: Davies, 1971); *The Overdeveloped Nations* (Swansea: Davies, 1977).

2. In Kohr, *The Inner City*, 127–139 (see note 1).

3. J. Jacobs, *The Economy of Cities* (New York: Random House, 1969). See also her most recent book entitled *The Nature of Economies* (New York: Random House, 2000).

4. In E. F. Schumacher, *Small Is Beautiful: Economics as If People Mattered* (London: Harper Perennial, 1989), p. 257. See also *This I Believe and Other Essays* (Totnes, UK: Green Books, 1997–1998).

5. E. F. Schumacher, "Centralization versus Decentralization," The Linisfarne Tape Series (Great Barrington, MA: Schumacher Society, 1974), 1-hour audio.

6. Ibid.

7. R. Laubacher et al., "Two Scenarios for Twenty-First Century Organizations: Shifting Networks of Small Firms or All-Encompassing Virtual Countries," WP 21CWP#001, Sloan School of Management.

8. "Letter to the CEO," *e-bizz*, <http://www.businessweek.com> (1999).

9. Small Business Administration, *The Third Millennium: Small Business and Entrepreneurship in the Twenty-First Century* (Washington, DC: U.S. Government Printing Office, available at <http://www.sbaer.uca.edu/docs/publications/pub00185.txt>.

10. See A. de Tocqueville, *Democracy in America* (2 vols., 1835), bk. 1, chap. 11. See at <http://books.mirror.org/gb.tocqueville.html>.

11. H. Henderson, *Development beyond Economism: Local Paths to Sustainable Development* (Great Barrington, MA: A. F. Schumacher Society, 1989.

12. C. Marinho, private e-mail message.

13. See, for instance, <http://www.seniornet.org>.

14. M. McFarland, "Humanizing the Information Superhighway," *IEEE Technology and Society Magazine* (Winter 1995–1996): 11–18.

15. See, for instance, more on the needs and assets of neighborhoods in A. Penzias, "The Next Fifty Years: Some Likely Impacts of Solid-State Technology," *Bell Labs Technical Journal* (Autumn 1997): 155–168.

16. R. Keohane and J. Nye, "Power and Interdependence in the Information Age," Harvard JFK School Lecture Series (1999).

17. F. Cairncross, *The Death of Distance* (Boston: Harvard Business School Press, 1998).

18. OECD, "A Global Action Plan for Electronic Commerce" (Paris, October 1999).

Index

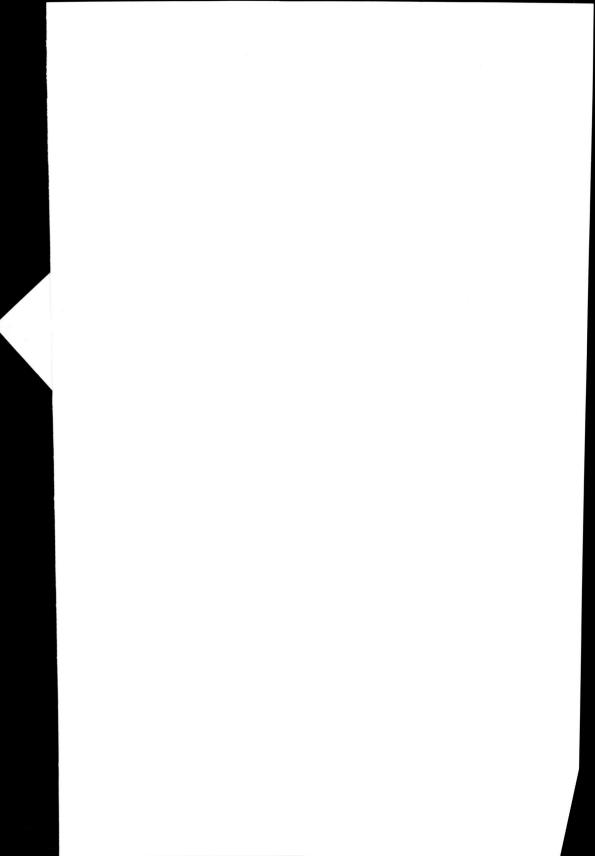